Spiritual Advice to the Hip, Slick, and Cool

Chuck Young

Marla McDowell-Young

Copyright © 2011 Marla Mc Dowell

All rights reserved.

ISBN: 0692210555
ISBN-13: 978-0692210550

DEDICATION

My husband and I want to thank God for giving us the wisdom and inspiration to write this wonderful book.

We also want to thank Monica McDowell, Phyllis McDowell-Junor, Acacia Kuykendall (on the cover), Ronnie Saeed Robinson (on the cover), and Basim Zahir, for their support. Saeed is now with God. May his soul rest in peace.

CONTENTS

INTRODUCTION

PROLOGUE

STORY 1 ABUSE   1

STORY 2 ANGER   18

STORY 3 BEHIND BARS   25

STORY 4 FAMILY VALUES   37

STORY 5 GAMBLING   42

STORY 6 GANG BANGIN'   47

STORY 7 GENERATION X   54

STORY 8 JUST BECAUSE YOU SEE MY TEETH   69

STORY 9 PLAYERS   72

STORY 10 MY RELATIONSHIP/FRIENDSHIP   80

STORY 11 SELF HATE   84

STORY 12 FREE WILL   95

EPILOGUE

CLOSING REMARKS

PROLOGUE

SPIRITUAL WARFARE FOREVER EXISTS

Through the grace of God my husband and I were chosen to write this book. God blessed us with Wisdom, Insight, Encouragement and Determination so that we could accomplish this endeavor.

My husband received the imagination for the topic of this wonderful book while being incarcerated due to the use of drugs and alcohol. While fighting the demon of Spiritual Warfare, God entered into his spirit and took over his soul. God also saved him from spending a great deal of time behind bars, I believe, in order for the information in this book to be read by the younger generation and generations before them.

With both of our life experiences we were able to accomplish, what we feel, will help mankind to understand what motivates the struggles in life. Fortunately during my lifetime I learned to type and took writing courses in college, which enabled me to write the book in a form of language that could be understood by all generations.

I always wanted to be a writer. I believe it is my calling. In the past I began writing a book, but never finished it. To be truthful, I never finished anything of any importance in my whole lifetime, which is one of the reasons why I was so determined to finish this book. Which I believe is God's will.

In the event of writing the book all of its contents were mysteriously lost in the computer never to be retrieved, no matter what measures we took. We were in the midst of writing the seventh chapter when the information of the book was lost. It blew our minds. We both became very depressed because we had worked so hard. While trying to retrieve the document we argued, blamed each other for the loss, and blamed the devil for our misfortune.

Fortunately we had our notes and taped recorded information, so we started all over again. I promised myself and my husband that I would type a portion of the book every day, no matter what. Through the grace of God, in a short period of time, once again the book came alive and was even better than the first addition. We than began to believe that God erased the first addition from the computer in order for us to make the second one even better. We believed that we were being tested by God for our patience and endurance.

Meanwhile, in the midst of writing the second addition of the book, my husband was slowly being pulled back into the dark world of addiction. He became board and short tempered, and eventually the demon of anger slowly attacked my husband, and once again he picked up the habit of smoking cigarettes. He had given up the habit while incarcerated, and when he returned home he couldn't stand the smell of cigarette smoke, but Satan tempted him back into the habit. Satan also tempted my husband with alcohol which eventually also became a habit. At first he didn't enjoy either vice very much, but after using these drugs on a daily basis they soon became addictive.

God didn't want these poisons in my husband's temple, but his fleshly desires overcame him. Even though his spirit tried to fight off the temptation of these drugs being put into his system, even though he didn't enjoy them in the beginning, he continued to smoke and drink alcohol until eventually he returned to the use of crack cocaine. You see one addiction leads to another addiction.

At first my husband did not enjoy smoking crack cocaine either, and only used it once and a while, when that demon of anger kicked in. But drug addiction escalates. Once in a while turned into everyday use, and eventually he would stay up for a week at a time, smoking crack, until once again he became a full blown crack head.

My husband allowed Satan to take over his mind and his soul right at the time we were finishing the last chapter of the book. My husband allowed Satan to pull him away from the book through spiritual warfare, and manipulated his mind to focus on drugs, therefore removing God from being first and foremost in his life. In the beginning God was never out of focus in my husband's mind or soul, but he began straddling the fence between good and evil, battling with the concept of spiritual warfare.

Have you ever seen cartoons where a person has a devil on one shoulder and an angel on the other? This is how the concept of spiritual warfare works, your good spirit fights against your bad spirit. You have to choose which spirit rules your life, God or Satan. You may straddle the fence for a while, but you won't for long. Either your on Gods team or your on Satan's team, there is no in between.

Eventually my husband didn't even want to hear about the book and turned his back on anything pertaining to God. If I mentioned prayer, he didn't want to hear it. This is the same man who quoted scriptures from Bible at the wink of an eye. The same man who taught me not to speak with a foul mouth. The same man who didn't speak with a foul mouth. A man who praised the Lord as soon as he woke up in the morning, in the afternoon, and before he went to bed at night. A man who would not go out of the house without asking God to watch over him and protect him from this dark world. A man who respected me and treated me like a Queen. A man that put my wants and needs ahead of his own. This is a man who is familiar with spiritual warfare. A man who was in the process of writing a book on spiritual warfare. The same man who showed me the signs of spiritual warfare when I was being attacked by the evil one.

Yes, the devil attacked me with the demon of jealousy. The devil manipulated my mind into focusing on negative thoughts. I believed that my husband was messing around with every woman he encountered with. I accused him of having an affair with my neighbors (which were not his type or caliber), my sister, the clerks at the grocery store, the cashier at the video store, and any other woman that looked his way. All I could think about were his infidelities. I had no peace of mind. I thought I was going crazy.

This was at a time in our lives when my husband was the model of what an ideal husband would consist of. This was the time when God was first and foremost in our lives. The time in our lives when we attended church and kept our spirits positive. We spent almost every moment together. We loved being together, we were almost inseparable. He was as devoted to me as I was to him. He always gave me compliments, kept me happy and made me laugh. He always showed and communicated how much he loved me. My husband had so much love for me that when he told me he loved me, his eyes would tear up. This was when our relationship was solid.

You see Satan attacks you when you are happy and content. He knows your weaknesses and plays on them. Jealousy happened to be mine and drugs were my husbands. The devil attacked me first, but thanks to God I caught on and eventually understood what was taking place. I realized that I was being put through a test. I realized that God is in charge of everything and he was allowing Satan to take me through spiritual warfare. You see you have to walk the walk in order to talk the talk. God took me to school so that I could feel the wrath of spiritual warfare. Satan was trying with all his might to drive a wedge between my husband and myself before we finished the book. Satan did not want the information on spiritual warfare to reach Gods children.

My husband told me that I had to get a grip on myself. Eventually he too understood what was taking place. So we turned to our father and asked for his mercy. We prayed that he remove the negative thoughts from my mind. I had to prove to God that I knew in my heart that he could and would remove Satan's lies from controlling my thoughts. God heard our prayers and cleared my mind from Satan's grips.

Satan kept my husbands mind focused on negetivity and drugs, rather than focusing on the book, which drove a wedge between him and I. You see my spirit hated what my husband's spirit had become. He had become physically, mentally, emotionally and verbally abusive, self centered, angry, violent and disrespectful. Drug abusers care about one thing only, and that is the use of drugs, and obtaining them by any means necessary.

People who live with drug addicts go through hell. Be it the wife, girlfriend, husband, boyfriend, mother, father or friend. A drug addict has a one track mind. All they concentrate on is their next hit. They become liars, thieves and abusers, even if it is not in their nature. My husband made me give him money, took from me, called me every name in the book at any given time, bullied and intimidated me. He didn't care about anyone but himself. I had to hide my money and eventually couldn't have money in the house.

I had to walk on tip toes due to his paranoia. I was completely uncomfortable in my own home. He would take the car (we only had one) and keep it for days at a time, preventing me from going to work. Eventually I would stay away from home as long as possible, because I couldn't stand the sight of him.

I cried day and night. I was never happy. I was lonely, depressed, and an emotional wreck. I aged 5 years and had bags and black rings under my eyes. You see our spirits continuously clashed. My holy spirit of God hated what he had become and his evil spirit of Satan hated my holy spirit. We argued all of the time about any and everything. Every move I made had a motive to it. If I tied my shoe he suspected something. I was living a life so stressful that it had become unbearable. I didn't like him around when he was under the influence, which was most of the time. The only time I liked him around was when he was asleep. I lived in fear, fearing for my life on a daily basis. My husband had a Doctor Jackal, Mr. Hide personality. His normal personality is calm, cool, and collective. But drugs and alcohol make him violent and extremely mean.

I became more and more depressed. "Spiritual Warfare" the devil didn't want us to finish the book, and was trying with all his might to break us apart. Eventually I gave into the devil. I cried to my husband, telling him how I felt like using drugs myself and that I felt suicidal. You see I have a history of drug abuse also. So one day I allowed Satan to drive me into doing drugs once again, due to depression and due to the love I had for my husband. Like they say, if you can't beat them, join them. I had been clean for over two years because of God's will. But I gave into drugs to try and keep peace within my marriage. Hoping that keeping him company would help us.

It didn't. We became further apart. We never had peace. Even when we got high we were not happy. That's because God didn't want us happy while under the influence. Our relationship became worse and we grew further apart. We didn't trust one another, always argued, and were verbally abusive to each other. We lived in a world that was like being in hell. We both allowed Satan to take over our lives. So we thought!

I thought that I was at the breaking point of my life. I thought that I was heading for a nervous breakdown. I felt that I was going to die of a heart attack or have a stroke due to stress. But deep down in my heart I also knew that God would not give me more than I could bare. I knew in my heart that my husband truly loved me, and that he too would eventually fight the temptations of the devil. We both were sick, but I knew God would take us out of the hell in which we lived. I knew in my heart, which is where God lies, that one day everything would be good. We straddled the fence for a while, but eventually we both chose to be on God's team. We both came to realize that we were still living in the realms of **SPIRITUAL WARFARE**!

GOD IS IN CHARGE

All that we went through was in God's plan. You must realize that your life was planned out for you before you were conceived. After getting clean and allowing our brains to function normally, we both realized that God is in charge of Satan. We realized that our father was showing us and taking us through Spiritual Warfare, so that we would recognize the depths, and what pain and suffering it causes. God wanted us to come to him, to rely on him. We didn't have to go through hell; we chose to go through it. All of Gods children are blessed with a gift, which is "Free Will". We all have the power to choose good over evil.

As you can see, Gods will was finalized and we finished the book. Through our pain and suffering we were able to do Gods work, and God is going to be glorified through us.

You must realize the impact that Spiritual Warfare has in our lives. We pray that this book helps you to recognize Spiritual Warfare first hand. Remember that it's an everyday battle to choose between good and evil. And also remember that any and all of Life's encounters and endeavors can be conquered by believing in or Lord and Savior Jesus Christ, and having faith by trusting in our Father God.

INTRODUCTION

SPIRITUAL ADVICE TO THE HIP, SLICK AND COOL

Welcome to the world of **Hip, Slick and Cool.** Welcome to a world driven by power, control, diversion, manipulation, lies, deceit, division, and lust. A world manipulated by the Devil. My wife and I wrote this book in order to awaken **Gods** children to the evils of this world. This world which has everyone blinded into believing that the love of money, the root of all evil, is more important than having faith in **God.** This world that is driven by a force which places illusions in your mind by feeding it negative energy and negative thoughts, while making you believe that living foul will make your life complete.

My wife and I would like to inform you that life is a gift from **God,** and the way you live your life will show **God** how grateful you are for that gift. **Jesus Christ** came into the world to show us how to live our lives in order for us to make it back to our heavenly home. For **Jesus** is the way, the truth and the life. You must realize that faith is the key, and you must put your faith in him.

Satan's desire is to put us in a satanic prison, and to also put us in a self imposed prison that attacks us spiritually, physically, mentally, and intellectually. Satan wants to be number one in our lives, and therefore desires us to worship him. So remember when Satan attacks, pray to **God** for strength to fight off his temptations. Prayer changes every situation from negative into positive. Read your Holy Bible. Study the word of **God.** Verbalize, meditate, and memorize the scriptures of the Bible.

Satan, who is the unseen enemy of this world, paints a picture in your mind that being **Hip, Slick and Cool** is the way to live your life, when in reality being **Hip, Slick and Cool** is an illusion designed by the evil one to destroy your life. The enemy's sole purpose is to keep you blinded from the evils of this world, therefore making it as hard as possible for you to make it back home. **God** gave us all free will, which gives you the choice to choose good over evil, life over death. The battle between the spirit of **God** and the spirit of the Devil is the concept of **Spiritual Warfare.** Choose your path wisely.

HIP, SLICK AND COOL

Being **Hip, Slick and Cool** is an artificial strength, an illusion of grander designed by the evil one. The evil spirit of **Hip, Slick and Cool** prays on the insecure, the weak, people with low self esteem, no self worth, people who have the need to be a part of something, people who have the need to be noticed, people with huge egos, the famous, the rich, the abused, the lonely, and the list goes on and on.

Satan attacks you when you feel good about yourself, when something positive is happening in your life, and you therefore take life for granted. He attacks when you believe that you are in control of your fate, when you have that me, me, and me attitude. I'm so smart, I'm so talented, I'm so good looking, I'm so **Hip, Slick and Cool.** He attacks you when you take **God's** gifts for granted. He attacks you when you are alone. As it is written: An idle mind is the devils workshop.

Hip, Slick and Cool, (designed by the evil one to destroy your life), paints the illusion in your mind that glorifies selling drugs, using drugs, pimping, prostituting, gambling, hustling, gang bangin, lying, cheating, using foul language, disrespecting others, good looks, being sexy, participating in adultery, driving fast cars, and the bling-bling. **Hip, Slick and Cool** paints the illusion that foul living will make your life complete. It paints an illusion that the more money you have the happier you will be, the more status you have, the more important you are, the more material items you possess, the more attention you'll receive.

SPIRITUAL WARFARE

Spiritual Warfare began in Heaven. Satan and his Angels tried to overthrow **God** and were therefore cast down to earth. Satan wanted to be equal to **God.** Therefore, if Satan was able to manipulate Angels who were in the presence of **God** to follow him, how much of a chance do we have as human beings on earth, to resist his lies, deceit, and temptations?

Spiritual Warfare does exist. It consists of two spirits that are designed to persuade you to have positive or negative energy. You will either live your life in a **godly** manner or an un-**godly** manner. There is a constant battle between the two spirits, which pulls you between light and darkness, good and bad, righteous and evil.

Realize that there is a force within this world that you cannot see. This force is strong and pulls you to do evil. All human beings have an empty hole inside them, a void that seems as if it cannot be filled. If you do not fill that void with the spirit of **God** it will remain empty, and the evil one will continue to fill it with foulness. You are either on **God's** team or the Devils team. There is no in between. The key is that you have the power to choose how you will live your life. For **God** gave all his children "free will".

Certain people are chosen by **God** to be trained. They go through life's hard knocks, scrapes and falls. **God** gives them the strength to fight the battle of good versus evil, and how to win. Some make it down the block, some don't make it.

THE SPIRIT OF JESUS CHRIST

The Spirit which produces love, joy, peace, patience, kindness, goodness, faithfulness, humility and self control, belongs to **Christ Jesus**. The spirit of **Jesus** has given us life, therefore he must also control our lives. The spirit of the **Lord** is the light that is inside us. Everyone won't open their hearts to the light. Everyone is not designed to receive the light. The light is from within, from the love in your hearts. The light is love. **God** is love.

The Unseen Enemy (The Evil Spirit)

We are consumed by evil forces; evil forces that cannot be seen by the human eye, evil forces that drive you into the darkness. If you are not aware of these evil forces they will drive you into making choices which will destroy your life. The forces are cunning and baffling. The evil spirit will manipulate your mind, making you believe you can get away with doing evil. Making you believe that you call the shots.

Then, just when you feel like everything is going your way, and that you are on top of the world, the devil changes your course, and before you know it your world is turned upside down. The evil one will set a trap for you by making you believe that you are untouchable; making you believe that you cannot be hurt.

So you walk around being the big man or women. Through manipulation money comes easy to you. You feel bigger than life, therefore developing the habit of disrespecting people. But then you run into the wrong one. You get shot for saying something out of line. You in turn shoot the person who harmed you, (kill them). You go to jail for the rest of your life, wondering what happened, not understanding what took place to turn your life upside down. Or the ultimate happens, and the forces of evil trick you out of your life. No matter how much money you stacked up, when the smoke clears, you must pay for those ill-gotten gains. Which more than likely ends in disaster.

Be aware!! You can sense when the devil is manipulating your mind. You will hear evil thoughts in your head and wonder where they came from. You can feel evil upon you. It's an uneasy feeling, an uncomfortable feeling, a feeling of despair, a feeling that makes you sad. If it doesn't feel right, it's not right. If it feels like a force is driving you to do wrong, it is.

How To Win The Battle Of The Evil Spirit

Satan misleads us, guides us in the wrong direction, and then deceives us. To win the battle of the evil spirit you must claim the blood of **Jesus Christ**. Claiming his blood will give you protection from the evil one. If you believe in **Jesus Christ**, you will receive his mercy. Depend on **God** to help you to overcome sinful thoughts. Call on him to hold your hand and allow yourself to overcome the temptations of the evil one.

The Devil cannot make you do anything. All he can do is extend an invitation that looks good. Satan distracts your focus of positive thinking and drives you to focus on foolishness. Satan is not in control. He is a liar, a thief, a manipulator, and a deceiver. If you resist him, he will resist you. The more you rely on **God**, the less power Satan has over you.

God has a plan for you that is greater than any money, status or material items of this world, which is life in an eternal paradise and everlasting peace. Be a light in this dark world!!

The Flesh

The Flesh is our human nature. The flesh is opposed to what the **Godly** spirit wants. The two are enemies and this means that you cannot do what you want to do in life. Instead you must allow **God's** word to guide you through life. The flesh is weak. It is sinful and is a negative energy that wants to do the things that makes it feel good. The flesh is made from dirt, therefore it is automatically dirty. Which is why it is easier to put the light out from within ourselves, rather than battle with the darkness around us.

Most human beings put the light out that's inside themselves and join the darkness around them. In the game of darkness there are no rules. The game of **Hip, Slick and Cool** is the game of darkness, and it is designed by the devil.

SPIRITUAL ADVICE TO THE HIP SLICK AND COOL

Human Nature

Our human nature thrives on being **Hip, Slick and Cool.** It gives our flesh an oar of power and control. We believe that we as humans are in control, when we are not. We are in the power of **Spiritual Warfare**, good versus evil.

As it is written:
What human nature does is quite plan. It shows itself in immoral, filthy and indecent actions; in worship of idols and witchcraft. People become enemies and they fight; they become jealous, angry, and ambitious. They separate into parties and groups; they are envious, get drunk, have orgies and do other things like these.

Also human nature thrives on corruption, deceit, shows falsehood, ingratitude, moral decay, sexual perversion, adultery, immortality, and the list goes on and on.

Protect your Eyes and Ears

When you become the age where you have to deal with the world, you become consumed by darkness and negativity, such as: smoking, drinking, foul language, drug use, joining gangs, attending strip bars, get rich quick schemes, being materialistic, conceit, prostitution, jealously, greed, theft, and every other foul thing you can think of.

These acts of negativity pull you into the mind frame of **Hip, Slick and Cool.** Like a pie, it looks good on the outside, but you don't know what's inside until you cut it open. Also like a pie, most of these elements look good on the outside, but when you cut them opened they are filled with poison. They are all illusions that are designed by the evil one to sway you away from the light within, which is the spirit of **God.**

Have you ever been sitting around, minding your own business, when an evil thought enters into your mind? Be aware that the enemy has access to your mind. The evil one will suggest evil thoughts, take that negative thought, and turn it into a motion.

For example: The evil one will trick you into selling drugs or doing other foul acts, which leads to incarceration. You therefore leave your wife or girl friend alone to fend for themselves. You then lose your home and your car gets repossessed. If the wife or girlfriend is also involved, she goes to jail also. The children end up in foster homes, and before you know it your life is in total chaos. In some instances you may get killed due to living foul. The devil has therefore accomplished his goal. He has destroyed a family and/or taken your life.

Don't be fooled by the devil. Listen to your heart. **God** is in your heart. The light from within is the spirit of **Jesus Christ**. Follow the light, even though it's hard to do in this dark world driven by evil forces.

It is not our words, the **Lord** says: Do not marvel at wrong doers, for I the **Lord** will cut them down like grass.

STORY 1

SPIRITUAL WARFARE/ABUSE

We as human beings have all experienced abuse of some sort in our life time. There is no way of avoiding it. We were either physically, verbally, mentally, emotionally or sexually abused. We have also in some way or fashion harmed ourselves by abusing drugs, alcohol, self mutilation, and the list goes on and on.

Global Abuse

Man not only abuses himself and his fellow man, he also abuses the world as a whole. Man abuses the air in which affects the ozone layer. He abuses the oceans where our water supplies lye. Man abuses the plant life and the rain forests. Man also abuses the wild life. In reality the entire world is affected by abuse. Only **God** can save us!

Believe it or not abuse is a negative energy designed by the evil one to destroy lives. Remember that any energy that is not positive is a negative energy, and that all negativity comes from the devil. We must never forget that **God** is love and therefore wants all of his children to be happy. We live our lives in an ongoing battle between good and evil, which is the concept of **Spiritual Warfare**.

Abuse in Relationships

If you are a woman or a man who is experiencing verbal, mental, emotional, physical and/or sexual abuse in a relationship, get out of that relationship. You must realize that the abuser is not in control of his or her actions.

Realize that they are being manipulated by the evil one, and are allowing the devil to control his or her mind by feeding it foulness. Satan does not want you happy. His sole purpose is to manipulate your mind with evil thoughts and desires in order to drive you into performing evil acts upon yourself and others.

If the word of **God** is not included in your relationship it is destined to fail. There will always be disagreements in relationships. The key is that you take a good look at yourself in order to resolve your problems. Use a spiritual concept of remaining positive to resolve conflicts. Worrying turns into fear, and fear into anger, and anger can result into abuse. Confide in **God**, he will take away all of your troubles. For **God** is in control of everything.

Physical Abuse

If you are being physically abused, and the abuser promises you that he or she will stop, don't go for the Okey Doke. Don't believe they will stop abusing you without help. How many instances have you heard about where an abuser beats the abused unrecognizable? After the beating the abuser cries and begs for forgiveness for what they have done. They may even have a sincere feeling of sorrow for what they have done. So time after time the abused forgives the abuser, and in the meantime the abuse becomes more and more violent. But the abused stays in the relationship and continues to receive the beatings, hoping one day that they will stop. But they don't stop. Then one day the abuser gets angry to the extreme where they disfigure the abused for life by punching out an eye, pulling out plugs of their hair, busting teeth out of their mouth, breaking bones, or setting them on fire, and eventually killing them. In such cases the evil one has accomplished his ultimate desire. He has tricked another person by manipulating their mind to do evil, which eventually resulted into taking someone's life.

Verbal Abuse

The pain of verbal abuse cuts deep into your soul. The saying – sticks and stones may break my bones, but words will never hurt me – so not true. Verbal abuse causes emotional abuse, mental abuse, and physical abuse. Which leads to drug abuse and alcohol abuse. When being verbally abused over and over again in life, especially by someone you love or care about, the abused soon begins to believe the negativity that is being fed into their minds. The abuser makes the abused feel small, shallow, unwanted, unattractive, and unloved. Which causes the abused to have low self esteem, no self worth, and no drive in life. After being told over and over again that they are unworthy and nobody wants or desires them, they soon begin to believe it. Sooner or later they begin to feel that they are not worthy to be alive, and in some circumstances will take their own life.

Verbal abuse is sometimes characterized as being **Hip, Slick and Cool**. In this day and age using the word "Nigga" is considered **Hip, Slick and Cool**. In the black culture this degrading word is used to show unity, friendship, and a since of belonging. Some people use this word before every sentence that comes out of their mouth. But it doesn't stop with black people; it is used by all nationalities because the youth of today feel saying this word is **Hip, Slick and Cool**. People – Do some research and read what this degrading word represents. Do some soul searching and remember how our forefathers were in slaved, beaten, killed, raped, disrespected, and treated like animals while their slave masters used this degrading word for the sole purpose of making them feel inferior.

Back in the day, not too long ago, and even today, if this word is used for the attempt to disrespect someone, the person using this word is in for a fight. The youth of today feel that the word Nigga and the word Nigger have two different meanings. They feel Nigga is OK to use, that it's a **Hip, Slick and Cool** word. But Nigger is a racist word. When in reality both words have the same exact meaning. The word is an insult, along with words like, kyke, wet back, white trash or trailer trash, Buda head and genie.

Other degrading words commonly used today are the words Bitch and Whore (hoe). Men use these words in order to disrespect women and women use them to disrespect each other. Sadly, women also use these words when addressing each other. In some instances these words are also labeled as **Hip, Slick and Cool**.

On the other hand these words can be used as in insult, such as: Ugly bitch, stupid bitch, sorry bitch, and so on. The words slut, bitch, and whore are mimicked as **Hip, Slick and Cool** on television programs as well as in certain music of today. Look up these words in the dictionary and see what they represent.

Would **God** call you any of these degrading names? Of course Not! So where do you think these foul use of words came from? Who do you think manipulates your mind in order for these foul words to come out of your mouths? – Satan! Using foul language and foul name calling is a moral decay of your own spiritual existence.

Verbal abuse is another strong source of negativity. An evil manipulating emotion brought on by the evil one. Remember, the devil will manipulate your mind with negative energy if you don't have the **Holy Spirit** to protect it. The more you rely on **God,** the more protection you will receive from him.

As it is written: It is not what goes into your mouth that makes you ritually unclean, rather what comes out of it makes you unclean.

Sexual Abuse

Do not exclude anyone from having the desires of sexual perversion. A sexual abuser can be your husband, wife, child, neighbor, teacher, friend, uncle, aunt, brother, sister, mother or father, a grandparent, and of course a total stranger. In many instances men and women who represent themselves as being messengers of **God's** word are in reality sexual predators. Such as: pastors, ministers, priests, rabbis, and nuns. Many men and women who would be considered as people with high status can also be sexual abusers. Such as: government officials, judges, doctors, lawyers, and the list goes on and on.

Sexual abusers are more than likely power seekers. They get off from the thrill of control and fear in most cases, rather than the actual act of sexual gratification. In many cases rapists are the most violent sexual abusers. They are brutal, vicious and animalistic. They usually not only sexually abuse their victims, but beat them, stab them, bite them, strangle them or shoot them to death. They too are in the battle of **Spiritual Warfare**. They are under the spell of the evil one.

In some instances they feel sad and disgusted with themselves. They wish they didn't have such foul, selfish, demeaning, and unnatural desires. In many instances the sexual abuser will take his or her own life, because they don't know how to stop the evil one from manipulating their minds into being predators of sexual abuse.

The sexual abuser must realize that they cannot stop the desire of sexually abusing others on their own. They must turn their lives over to **God,** through **Jesus Christ**. They must repent their sins and trust in **God**. There is no other way to stop their evil ways. Either you're on **God's** team or you're on Satan's team. There is no in between.

Child Sexual Abuse

In my opinion the worse abuse that's ever taken place on this earth is child sexual abuse, or the seduction of children. Children are so innocent. They are so trustworthy and pure. It is such a misfortune that people pry on their innocence by obstructing sexual abuse upon them. In many cases children are abducted by strangers. But sadly, in most cases, the abuser is a family member, neighbor, teacher, doctor or friend of the family. The abuser is commonly someone whom the child trusts; therefore the child believes this person will not do anything to harm them.

When a child is sexually abused by someone they know, it is usually initiated when the child is around 3 – 7 years of age. The predator starts off by grooming the child, in other words gaining their trust. They find out through manipulation the likes and dislikes of the child. The predator makes the child feel as if they can trust them more than they trust their own parents. They manipulate the child's mind making them believe that they are more understanding than their parents. The predator also manipulates children by being extremely nice to them, by bribing them with animals, money, gifts and candy.

After the grooming period, the predator begins the seduction of the child. They may start off by fondling the child. At first the child feels uncomfortable because they feel in their heart that what is taking place is wrong. The child feels that this person should not be touching them on their private parts. But being that they fear or even worse trust this pedophile, they give them the benefit of the doubt. This pervert manipulates the child into believing this act is normal, and that it's a secret that only they share. In some instances the predator threatens to kill the child as well as their family members if this secret is not kept between the two of them.

Eventually, in some cases, depending on who the predator is, the child begins to relax when being molested because of the way the seduction takes place. If the abuser only fondles the child it begins to feel good to them (in some cases). If the predator is gentle, the child enjoys the feeling of being touched, licked, and sucked on their private parts. Therefore they cooperate and in some instances even look forward to the next encounter of the sexual seduction. In some cases these children become promiscuous enjoying sex at an early age.

On the other hand, you have perverts who take nude pictures of young children, and at times encourage them to have sex with other young children, while taking pictures of them in indecent positions. You also have sexual perverts who expose young children committing these indecent sex acts on the internet to make money by featuring these young children to other perverts and pedofiles.

Sadly you also have sexual maniacs who have sex with children sometimes under the age of six. These perverts are into inflicting pain upon children while abusing them mentally, emotionally and physically. Featuring pictures on the internet with children being tied and handcuffed onto a bed while being raped. Screaming in pain with agony written all over their faces. Many of these child abuse maniacs are into beating, strangling and stabbing these innocent children, and eventually killing them. These child molesting low life's are being driven by the evil one, and aren't even aware of it.

Most sexually abused children as they become older, realize that what is taking place is wrong. They realize that this encounter is not normal. When the child becomes 6 – 12 years of age the abuser usually begins sexual intercourse. In some cases the pedophile forces the sexual act on the child on a regular basis. At this point in their life the child most likely develops serious emotional, mental, and physical problems. Some children when being molested, condition their thoughts to another place and time. Pretending as if the sexual act is not happening. This act of protection can cause the child to develop multiple personalities.

At some point the child wants to inform someone of what's going on, but feels like it is their fault for allowing this horrible situation to continue for so long. In some instances, when a girl child is being molested by her father, step father or mother's boy friend, the child tries to tell her mother that she's being sexually abused. Sadly, in many cases, the mother is in denial and won't listen to the child when they complain about the sexual abuse. And even more sadly, at times, the mother blames the child for the sexual encounters.

In some cases, when a girl child informs her mother, the mother ignores the child, and therefore allows the abuse to continue because she doesn't want to have conflict with the man in her life causing him to run off and leave her. She doesn't want to be alone, and for her own selfish desires allows this Pedophile to continually sexually abuse her daughter. There have been many children who have given birth to babies fathered by their fathers, stepfathers or mothers boyfriends. Unfortunately predators and sexual abusers don't stop with little girls. The same degrading sexual encounters happen to young boys. In fact young boys are targeted more often than young girls.

If the child doesn't share this horrible secret with someone, in many instances they eventually develop even more serious psychological problems. In many circumstances these sexually abused children molest children younger than themselves, or end up in juvenile hall, become prostitutes, gay, have trust issues in relationships, have difficulties with sexual intercourse when in relationships, have extremely low self esteem, and become ruined emotionally for life. Some children end up taking their own lives. If they make it to adulthood, and haven't been saved by the **Lord Jesus Christ**, many end up being child sexual abusers themselves, and menaces to society.

Meanwhile, this devil driven predator continues to sexually abuse this child. This pervert who is being manipulated by the evil one continues to commit foul acts on this child, wondering why he or she does it. This Pedophile who is so weak as an adult, can only feel power by manipulating young children. This sexual manipulation makes them feel slick as if they are getting away with something. There is nothing **Hip, Slick and Cool** about causing pain to a child. This sorry excuse of a human being is caught up in the tug of war of **Spiritual Warfare,** and is not even aware of it.

Who in their right mind would desire a child sexually? Being in the grips of **Spiritual Warfare** is no joke. The evil ones mission is to destroy lives, at any cost, no matter how young the victim is.

Fortunately there are sexually abused children who are strong in mind and spirit that have overcome sexual abuse, and have grown up to live normal lives. Many have become prosperous, and even famous in life. But be aware that it was **God's** grace that saw them through, and **God's** grace that granted them peace of mind to move on with their lives. But through it all, at any given time, they can reflect back to when the abuse took place. The key is, that they are able to shut off the memories that exist for the rest of their lives.

Unfortunately, child sexual abuse is an enormous epidemic which is the way of life in some cultures, that is handed down from generation to generation. Also, unfortunately in today's society, child sexual abuse is out of control. The children targeted seem to be younger and younger. **"Only God can save them"**

Words of Wisdom

Children: You must keep your antennas up and your eyes and ears open. If you suspect that someone is paying too much attention to you where it doesn't seem normal, no matter who that someone is, tell, tell, tell someone. Let someone whom you love and trust know that you don't feel comfortable around that individual.

Recognize the signs of the grooming period, which consists of, bribery, too much hugging, slightly touching you on the wrong places, and mind games. Don't allow anyone to isolate you or spend too much alone time with you. Remember: If it doesn't feel right, it's not right.

If you are a child who has already experienced being groomed by a predator, or have been seduced, sexually abused, raped or molested, and you are keeping the situation to yourself, you too must also tell, tell, tell someone. Free yourself from the grips of the predator as soon as possible. Do not blame yourself or feel guilty about the sexual rape. **IT IS NOT YOUR FAULT!**

If you are a parent you must protect your children. Inform them at an early age that no one is suppose to inappropriately touch them on their private areas, teach them that it is not OK. Not by anyone. Not friends of the family, teachers, clergymen, siblings, a parent or even a grandparent. **NO ONE!**

You must develop a relationship with your children where they will feel comfortable talking to you about any issue. Don't judge them. Put yourself in their place. Remember how it was when you were their age. We all go through the same issues during adolescent. Love, nurture, and respect your children. Poor as much love upon them as you can. You can never love them too much.

Don't spoil your children with material items. Give them humanly love, quality time, and patience. Explain to your children when they are old enough about the struggle of the flesh and human nature. Teach them that being **Hip, Slick and Cool** is not a priority in their lives. Explain to them about **Spiritual Warfare**, the battle between good and evil.

Reach them while they are young. Make them aware of the evil one. Teach them that goodness, love, patience, joy, and kindness can only come from **God,** through our **Lord** and **Savior Jesus Christ**. Teach them how to pray to **God** every day, morning, noon and night, thanking him for all of their blessings. Teach them to be aware of how blessed they are.

Drug and Alcohol Abuse

The battle with drug and alcohol abuse usually begins during adolescent stages. The enemy creeps into young children's minds that are innocent, naïve and/or have low self esteem, and no self worth. Children who usually abuse drugs and/or alcohol are children who come from poor families, children who are slow at learning, children who are unloved, molested children, children from broken marriages, children whose parents abuse drugs, children from rich families who have easy access to drugs/alcohol, and the list goes on and on.

Children, as we adults, have that void, that empty feeling inside that we all try to fill with drugs, alcohol, eating, shopping, steeling, sex, and so on. We all have a feeling of emptiness inside that we as human beings cannot seem to fill, no matter how hard we try. As a matter of fact, the more we try to fill that void, the bigger the hole seems to become.

When children begin experimenting with drugs some children enjoy the effects of drugs and some don't. In some cases drug addiction is caused by a trait or gene handed down from generation to generation. Addiction usually attacks children with compulsive behaviors, children who are bored with life, children whom are followers, therefore are easily influenced, abandoned children, runaways, and of course innocent naive children who call themselves experimenting, and end up hooked.

Children usually start off abusing drugs by smoking cigarettes because it looks **Hip, Slick and Cool** to smoke. In some cases they graduate to smoking weed and drinking alcohol. Being that drug addiction escalates, in most cases they use other drugs such as, sniffing glue, sniffing paint, and drinking cough syrup. Drugs that are not so expensive. Eventually they escalate to the hard drugs. Such as: LSD, sherm, ecstasy, crack cocaine, meth, heroin, pharmaceutical drugs, and any other drug that they can get their hands on. Using any means necessary trying to fill that void, that emptiness inside. They are not aware that they are being manipulated by the evil one, and on their way to ruining their lives.

So you live your life doing drugs. It becomes the major part of your life. You have the false impression that you cannot function without them, that life sober is boring. People have the misconception that cigarettes are not a drug. WRONG - cigarettes, which consist of tar, nicotine, and many other toxic poisons is the hardest drug to kick. Weed smokers believe that marijuana is not addictive, when it is also very addictive. Pot heads wake up in the morning smoking blunts, and continue to smoke them all through the day and evening.

Some people are hooked on pills. They take an upper in the morning so that they can feel an artificial energy, and then a downer at night so that they feel relaxed and can go to sleep. Some people cannot function unless they have a drink the first thing in the morning, and continue to drink for the rest of the day until they have that last drink at night to help them sleep. The crack, meth and heroin addicts can go on all night. The crack and meth addicts can stay up for a week at a time, trying to fill that void.

When the crack and meth addicts finally pass out from exhaustion, they wake up and start all over again. Many addicts will overdose or commit suicide because they cannot stop using drugs and alcohol. The devil will manipulate you into a depressed state where you'll want to shoot your head off, jump off of a high building or cut your own throat, to free yourself from the prison of addition.

<u>Crack and Meth Abuse</u>

Crack and meth are mind altering drugs which make people extremely paranoid and unable to function normally. One hit alters the addict's personality. Their personality will change from being a kind and gentle person into a disrespectful monster, who will rob, steal, and kill for drug money.

Many crack and meth addicts spend all of their money on drugs. They don't pay rent, will live on the street, will not buy food, will eat out of garbage cans, and won't bathe. The female crack/meth addict won't spend their money on monthly female products. They would rather bleed all over themselves and smell like an animal, rather than spend their money on kotex or tampons, afraid that if they do that they will miss out on a hit.

On the other hand there are the so called functional drug addicts. These addicts have jobs which can range from janitorial to executive positions. These addicts go to work every day no matter how tired they are. They work during the day and stay up until the wee hours of the night or vice versa. If the addict's income is low, they will pay rent and utility bills, but the buck stops there. They spend the rest of their money on drugs. Clothes and material items are a no no. Every dime they can conger up will be spent on drugs.

There are also drug addicts whom are abundant in wealth that believe they can afford a crack or meth habit. Unfortunately, if they don't get a hold on themselves and their drug habit, they too will one day be broke. The more you smoke these extremely addictive drugs, the more you want them. No one can afford to be hooked on these drugs. If they don't become broke in the process of addiction, they will end up dead from an overdose, or lose their minds due to their brain cells being diminished, ending up institutionalized.

Nothing matters to these addicts except getting high. Some addicts due to the speed in their system may have the twisted mouth syndrome, where they cannot speak. There paranoia has them imagining someone's after them or something is crawling on them. They feel scared almost to death, feeling like they are going crazy. Satan manipulates their minds with negativity, making them have a delusional state of mind, which makes them depressed or violent because they believe negative activities are happening when they are not. They may also become schizophrenic, hearing and imagining seeing things that aren't really there. Even though these drugs make them uncomfortable and uneasy, even though they don't really enjoy the high. They turn around and take hit after hit, therefore going through the same ordeal over and over. Satan ain't no joke!

The addict at times takes on an animal like characteristic. After the brain cells have been damaged to the extreme of never being replenished, the addict takes on the look of a demon, and screams and makes satanic sounds because they are possessed by the devil.

You must realize that crack/meth addicts when under the influence, or after they have been brain damaged to the point of no return to function normally, are not in their right state of mind. Realize that they are under the influence of the evil one, driven by the evil spirit of Satan.

Men and women will not only sell their bodies, but will sell their children for a hit of crack or meth. Men who are normally straight will give other men oral and/or anal sex for these drugs. Women who are normally straight will sleep with other women, and do any undesirable sexual encounter you can imagine, in order to obtain these drugs.

Both crack and meth do extreme damage on one's body. These drugs not only eat up your brain cells, cause liver disease, heart problems, kidney problems, and affect your nervous system, but also take away from your outer beauty, causing a person to age faster than normal. These drugs eat up the calcium in your body causing your hair to fall out and your teeth to rot. If you've ever known a crack or meth head who has smoked for many years of their lives, they more than likely have several or all of their teeth missing.

Women will leave their children alone for days or weeks at a time, searching for a way to get money for another hit. They don't protect themselves from getting pregnant or contracting sexual diseases, and will in some instances have numerous crack/meth babies, which are more than likely put into foster homes. These children are addicted at birth to crack/meth, and have to go through withdrawals in order to kick the habit. They grow up slow to learn, unable to connect with other children or society, and in some cases are violent. Unfortunately, many of these crack/meth addicted babies are also born blind, deformed, and completely unable to function in life.

More than likely these crack/meth babies will become drug addicts and minuses to society themselves, at an early age. And sadly, in some cases, the cycle will continue from generation to generation. On the other hand many of these children who go through adolescence seeing what these drugs have done to their parents, will not touch drugs for the fear of growing up and being addicts themselves.

Be Aware

Don't let anyone influence you into taking one hit of crack, meth or heroin. One hit and you're hooked. Don't begin drug use by smoking cigarettes, drinking alcohol or smoking weed. Also be careful of the usage of pharmaceutical drugs, which too are very addictive.

Stay clear of anyone involved with these extremely addictive, deadly, mind altering drugs. Don't allow drug addiction to take you away from being the smart, beautiful, and amazing individual that **God** created you to be. Don't be robed of your potential.

Alcoholism

Many people are blinded by the perception that excessive alcohol use is not addictive because of its legality. That is the reason why there are so many alcohol addicts. Yes -Alcohol is a drug. When first consumed, like many drugs, alcohol makes you feel good, high, relaxed, happy, silly, and gives you the aura of being **Hip, Slick and Cool.**

In most cases children start of drinking alcohol by tasting their parents drinks, or by sneaking drinks from their parents bar or bottle, and by peer pressure. As any other drug, some children will enjoy the effects of drinking alcohol, some will not. Some children will grow up to be occasional drinkers, and some will become alcoholics.

Alcohol addiction like any other drug, escalates, which means that the more you drink the more your body craves. The more your body craves, the more you want. The more you consume, the higher you become.

People will lie, steal, rob, turn tricks, and kill in order to get another fix of alcohol. Alcohol has caused many people to lose their jobs, homes and material items of value. Don't be fooled into thinking that just because you can buy it in a store that it is not deadly.

Alcohol is also a mind altering drug. It makes most women feel happy and Horney, but tends to make men violent and disrespectful. It can also cause individuals to have blackouts when overly consumed.

There have been many occasions when women have gone to bed with strange men, and woke up in motel rooms not knowing how they got there. Not only that, but have waken up beaten and sore due to having sex with these complete strangers, and not remembering what took place. To top it off, find out that they have been robbed of their personal belongings, and robbed of their car. Or the ultimate happens, and they don't wake up at all, but are found dead in the hotel room, or end up dumped in a trash can by playing Russian Roulette with their lives.

Women and men will also take advantage of an alcoholic man. He might wake up in an alley not remembering how he got there. He too robbed and battered with no wallet in his pocket, with no car keys or car. An alcoholic man will come home to a happy house, beat and curse out his wife, beat the children, curse out the neighbors, and eventually curse out the police after they have been called. Ending up in jail, waking up sore and beaten, wondering what took place.

That's if he's lucky. There have been many instances when a drunk goes to the extreme of believing that they are untouchable and end up dead due to a consequence that happened, which wouldn't have if he or she were sober. When someone is under the influence of alcohol they take on a supernatural feeling. Feeling as if they can accomplish anything. This is why there are so many lives taken by drunk drivers.

Alcohol alters people's personalities. Many people with meek personalities drink because alcohol makes them outgoing. Some people cannot socialize without a drink; some people eventually cannot function without a drink. Alcohol is also considered the truth serum. There have been many friendships, relationships, courtships, etc., broken up due to an alcoholic full of the truth serum. Alcohol will make you tell people how you really feel about them, with nothing held back. Alcohol gives you an artificial courage, it makes you bold. Many a drunk has been brutally beaten up due to their foul use of language directed to another person while under the influence of alcohol.

Some people consume so much alcohol that they urinate on themselves and aren't even aware of it. It is not attractive watching an alcoholic stagger, fall, slur their words, spit when they talk, be rude, loud and disrespectful. Alcohol also tares the body down. It causes sclerosis of the liver, heart disease, diabetes, and many other deadly diseases. With excessive use it can make you look old beyond your years. Alcohol, if consumed in an enormous amount, takes away your dignity, and can take away your life due to the poisoning of the blood. Yes, you can overdose on alcohol.

Some people can drink moderately. That's OK. But if you find that you have a drinking problem or that you have a compulsive or addictive personality, leave the alcohol alone. "Beware" Anything that drives you into self destruction comes from the evil one. Anything that makes you happy, joyful and gives you peace of mind, comes from **God** through **Jesus Christ**.

Prescription Medication Drug Abuse

Prescription medication drug abuse has become a major problem in today's society. In my opinion it's more than likely been a problem for a long period of time, but society over looked it. I remember back in the day when I was in high school in the late 1960's, at a time when kids abused prescription medications, trying to fit in, trying to be **Hip, Slick and Cool**. Back then sleeping pills were called downers, which consisted of red devils, tuinols, valiums and yellow jackets. Uppers or speed consisted of diet pills, black mollies, whites and LSD.

I remember how downers made people slur their words and stumble around. I remember how they were unable to walk on their own without someone holding them up. I remember how young girls would be so completely out of it, that they would get raped and have trains pulled on them without even being aware of it. Luckily back then venereal diseases were curable, AIDS wasn't invented yet. Yes, I believe that AIDS is man made, but that would take another book to explain. I didn't understand why children would take those medications over and over again back then. Now I realize that they were addicted to them.

Even back then I remember people overdosing on the pills used for sleeping disorders. I also remember people accidentally killing themselves from taking an abundance of LSD. How they would hallucinate so badly that they would jump out of sky scraper windows, shoot themselves, stab themselves and others, and drown themselves, because they were not in control of their actions, and were not aware that they were in the realms of **Spiritual Warfare**.

Today pharmaceutical medication addiction is higher than it's ever been. Our society thrives on the consumption of prescription medications. Prescription drug addiction is a nationwide problem which is more common than the addiction of cocaine, heroin and ecstasy combined. They are also easier to purchase because you can buy them at drug stores, purchase them from prescriptions issued by your doctor, seek other doctors to prescribe them to you, and you can also purchase them on the inner net or on the street.

We as a society have so many social issues to deal with in this day and age. Many of us are in a continuous state of depression. Many of us are overweight or obese, and face pressures in life to be as thin as possible. Many hate the way they look, therefore have continuous cosmetic surgeries done over and over again. Some can't find work, which contributes to the loss of homes (foreclosures), homelessness, unruly children in the home, people living longer, racism, etc., so we choose to medicate ourselves in order to cover up our problems, to take away the pains of life.

But as all drug addictions, these prescription medications only add to the pain by altering personalities, attributing to violence, breaking up marriages and families, causing adultery, molestation, cheating, lying, loss of jobs, children addicted at birth, prostitution, robbery, sadness, more pain, anger, anxiety, loneliness, frustration, suicidal thoughts and attempts, self hate, low self esteem, hopelessness, sleeplessness. Using these drugs to try and fill that void in our lives, trying to fill whole.

Some of the popular and highly addictive prescription medications used today are: Valium (sleeping pill), Xanax, Vicodin, Morphine pills, Oxycodone (pain medications), which are potent and very addictive, and at times leads to heroin use because it's cheaper to purchase. And then you have Adder-all (used for attention deficit hyper disorder), which is straight speed.

Many prescription medication addicts become addicted by default, due to a legitimate illness where their doctor prescribes these drugs for pain, depression, insomnia or other illnesses. Then after taking these medications for a length of time, people begin to depend on the drug to help them cope with life, and after a period of everyday use, they begin to enjoy the effects of the drug. On the other hand, some people take these medications for the sole purpose of getting high. Many people take medications not prescribed for them, and end up hooked.

Prescription medications put you in the mind frame of **Hip, Slick and Cool.** They too are a product of Satan's temptations, manipulating your mind by feeding your fleshly desires. At first consumption many of these drugs give you a feeling that's so good; it's unexplainable. An hypnotic feeling, like the feeling of shooting heroin. Its better some say, than having an orgasm.

Then, when the addiction kicks in, you are no longer in control. Now you are hooked and your body needs the medication in order for you to function normally (so you think). **Spiritual Warfare** has taken over your life and you are not aware of it. You are now on Satan's team choosing evil over good. Any force that is not positive is negative, and all negativity comes from Satan. Satan's job is to destroy your peace and happiness by any means necessary.

These drugs as any other drug, escalate in the use of consumption. At first 1 pill will do the trick, then you need 2, then 3, then 4, and so on. The more you ingest, the more your body wants, the more your body wants, the more you crave, until your addiction is completely out of control.

Do not abuse prescription drugs. Try not to depend on them for a long period of time. Be careful when they are prescribed for you. Especially medications prescribed for sleep disorders, pain medications, and medications for anxiety and depression. These drugs are highly addictive and cause serious problems to your body. Such as; high blood pressure, strokes, high pulse rates, heart attacks, clotting of the blood, commas, and can also cause overdose and death when overly consumed.

Conclusion

Drug abuse is a self conflicting disease, a death sentence. When you abuse your body with drugs and/or alcohol it is because you are being manipulated by the evil one to self destruct. An abuser cannot stop abusing others, and you cannot stop abusing yourself without help. Many have tried support groups or reading books on anger management, sexual perversion, eating disorders, and so on, only to fall back into the same abusive patterns.

Remember: **God, our Father,** gave all of his children the gift of **"free will".** This gift gives you the power to choose good over evil. The devil can only manipulate your mind if you allow him to do so.

Evil can only be conquered by giving oneself to **Jesus Christ,** and by confessing your sins to **God**. We as human beings have all experienced a feeling of emptiness inside, a void that we cannot seem to fill. So we choose alcohol, drugs, sex, and foul living in order to fill that void, only to continue feeling empty.

Only **Christ** can fill that void with his spirit of love, joy, kindness, happiness, and peace. You must repent your bad deeds and allow **God** to control your life. You must receive the **Holy Spirit** in your heart. The evil ones main objective is to manipulate your mind; **God** is in your heart. **God** is love. You will always be in the battle of **Spiritual Warfare**.

STORY 2

SPIRITUAL WARFARE/ANGER

Anger is a concept of **Spiritual Warfare** designed by the evil one to destroy you, your family, and others around you. Anger is a strong emotion which drives you to do evil, an emotion that can drive you into self destruction by encouraging you to disrespect, harm, harass, rape, devoir, and kill other human beings. Anger will give you desires to abuse alcohol, abuse drugs, pick up prostitutes, lie, cheat, deceive others, and conduct yourself in ways that aren't normal for you. Anger plays on your emotions. It allows the evil one to manipulate your thoughts and actions.

Anger also affects the family unit. If a couple argues constantly in front of their children, it can cause the children to become nervous and emotionally imbalanced. When parents lash out their anger onto their children, it leads to children becoming angry adults. For children learn by example.

As it is written: Be slow to anger, for anger will make you sin.

<u>Anger and foul language</u>

Anger and foul language usually go hand in hand. People who use foul language when angry consider themselves threatening, intimidating, and believe that they bring fear onto others. They haven't a clue that when they "curse somebody out" that they are being driven by the evil one with their mind frame in the concept of **Spiritual Warfare,** having no regard for someone else's feelings. They don't realize that the devil is manipulating their minds to harass, disrespect and degrade other human beings. Foul language is a source of verbal abuse and is not **Hip, Slick and Cool**.

SPIRITUAL ADVICE TO THE HIP SLICK AND COOL

Have you ever seen a person who looked good on the outside, was very attractive and well dressed, that seemed to have it all together? So you thought. Until they opened up their mouth and foul language came pouring out. Everything nice looking on the outside instantly diminished as soon as an array of four letter words began to spill out of their mouth. That same good looking person turned into a dressed up trash can with garbage flying out of its lid. Using foul language is not **Hip, Slick and Cool**. Instead it makes you look and sound ignorant, as if you have a limited vocabulary. Don't allow anger to play on your emotions.

Revenge

Anger can be used as a source for revenge. Revenge is a means of payback by someone whose heart has been broken, or by someone who has been embarrassed or disrespected in some way or another by someone they care about or can't stand the sight of. Nothing good comes out of revenge. Its intent is to harm someone else, when in reality you are harming yourself in the process. The person who has been hurt feels as if this act of malice will in turn make them feel better. When in reality being vengeful to someone usually makes matters worse.

Revenge can lead to destroying someone's life, and in turn destroying your own. People who seek revenge have only one thing on the brain, and that is causing pain, havoc, and destruction on another individual. You must remember that the devil is the product of evil desires; **God** is the product of love, joy, kindness, peace, and forgiveness. You must learn how to forgive. Learn how to make amends. Learn how to use your **Godly** instincts.

A woman scorned

A woman scorned is danger at it's peak. A woman whose heart has been broken, a woman who has been deceived, lied to, made a fool of, taken advantage of, and is mad about it, in most cases wants to do damage to her abuser by any means necessary. When a woman is in this state of mind the devil manipulates her thoughts to do as much harm to the one who hurt her as possible. Revenge is at the top of her list. She sees the color red. There is no stopping her from her destination of destruction. The evil one in turn manipulates her mind, causing it to conger up all sorts of evil activity.

In most instances when a woman goes crazy with revenge over a man, she has been madly in love with him. She loved him more than she loved herself. She took good care of him, gave him money, and anything else his heart desired, and devoted her life to him. He at one time in their relationship did the same, but lost the flame and found a hotter one. He then starts cheating, lying, and deceiving her. Because she's been so good to him he decides to keep her around to enjoy the pleasures of having two women. Thinking this way of life is **Hip, Slick and Cool.** When in reality he is in the grips of **Spiritual Warfare**, **Godly** desires versus evil desires.

He feels as if he has the best of both worlds until the day he gets caught. Remember, all that's in the dark will come into the light. Now he must choose which woman he wants to be with. In many cases both women will remain in the relationship, trying to see which one has the most clout, until one or the other gets tired of all the drama. The truth of the matter is, no matter who he chooses to be with or how long he juggles them both around, sooner or later he must face the wrath of a woman scorned.

On the other hand there are women who allow men to take advantage of them, knowing the man has no emotional ties to them. Knowing the man will never love them. She is aware that he is only using her, but she has low self esteem, and therefore buys him expensive material items, gives her body to him, and does whatever necessary to try and keep him around as long as possible. Just to be able to say that she has a man.

In return, he puts on an act as if he loves her, while showing no emotion for her. He never takes her anywhere, never buys her anything, gives her sympathy sex every now and then, if at all, and is hardly ever around. Throughout the relationship she is in denial, hoping one day that he will love and desire her. But it never happens. He gets more and more disrespectful until eventually he leaves her, and believes in his heart that he has gotten away clean. He actually believes that his mack was so strong that there will be no repercussions. He is under the illusion of **Hip, Slick and Cool.** An illusion that living foul makes him a big man. His mind is being manipulated by the evil one, and he is not aware of it.

Men who use women, break their hearts, and then leave them with no concern about their feelings are asking for trouble. After they have devastated these women do they really believe that they are going to get off easy? Do they believe they will get away with the hurt and pain that they have caused her? Do they actually believe that they can just walk away? In some instances they can just walk away. If a woman has good sense she will accept the fact that if someone doesn't want or love you, that it's time to move on.

But on the other hand some women hurt hard, especially when they feel they have been used and taken for granted. They sit at home crying their eyes out. Eyes swollen shut from crying day after day. They can't eat or they over eat. They can't sleep and can't function. Some women use drugs or alcohol to try and medicate the pain. Some even think about suicide. Some commit suicide. Some think about killing him!!

This is when the thought of revenge sets in. This is when **Spiritual Warfare** takes its course. It is written: A man would rather face a female bear with two of her cubs under each of his arms, than to face a woman scorned.

A woman scorned will make up lies to try and get the man that hurt her put in jail. She will call him over and over again, begging and pleading for him not to leave her; she will stalk him at home, at work, and leave threatening notes on his car and at his house. She will burn up, bleach, and cut up his clothes, shoes, and any other material items she can find. A woman scorned will throw bricks through car and house windows, key or set automobiles on fire. She will assault other females behind the man who hurt her. A woman scorned will stab, shoot, and kill a man behind her heart being broken. She will give up her life in order to pay back the man who hurt her, deceived her, and broke her heart.

A women scorned is not in her right state of mind when she commits these violent acts. She is being driven by the evil one, and is not aware of it. She is under an illusion, being driven to destruction by the devil. She herself cannot believe how she changed from a loving, devoted love mate, into a monster. Hopefully she will think about what she is doing and come back to reality. She must realize that this man is not the only man on earth. She must give herself credit and look deep within herself knowing in her heart that she can actually do better. Realize that she is worthy of being loved.

<u>When a man seeks revenge</u>

When a man seeks revenge extreme measures are usually the outcome. He becomes this monster that he himself didn't know existed. The acts performed on the victim are usually very violent. When a man's heart is broken the devil manipulates his mind to do harm on the one who hurt and disappointed him. Men hurt hard. All they see is red, bright red. They will get even with the one who broke their heart by any means necessary.

When a man is hurt by a woman (especially when he's given his heart and soul to her), it's hard for him to accept rejection or abandonment from her.

Being that most men are physically stronger than the average woman , they can more easily cause a woman bodily harm. Some men beat women when they are in relationships because they are insecure about their masculinity, therefore taking out their frustrations on their woman.

Then you have men who beat women because they were quit for another man or woman. The average man has no problem quitting a woman, but when the shoe is on the other foot, he can't handle it.

So she leaves him because she is tired of his playing around on her, tired of his verbal abuse, physical abuse and mental abuse. She's bored with him. He doesn't satisfy her sexually, or she just doesn't love him anymore. She's a woman about it; she tells him why she's leaving, that the relationship just isn't working out. He in turn acts hard about the situation, acts like he doesn't care. But in turn calls her all kinds of names, and throws her and her belongings out of the house (except for the things he bought for her). Because remember, he can't handle rejection.

She's gone. Loneliness sets in. No matter how many other woman he has or doesn't have, at this point and time she is all that matters. She is all that he thinks about. He calls her on the phone over and over again, leaving message after message. She doesn't accept or return the phone calls; she doesn't want to be bothered. The messages start of nice, he begs for her forgiveness. Then they become arrogant and finally threatening. When he realizes that she is not going to return his calls, the stalking begins. His mind is set to believe, "If I can't have her, nobody can".

At this point the devil has him. He is not thinking on his own. He starts following her around. If he sees her out with another man there are no questions asked, he'll just proceed to beating them both up (If he can), and anytime he catches her alone, she's in for a beating. After the smoke clears and he realizes what he has done, he hates himself for how he's behaved. Then the tears come and he begs the woman for forgiveness. When that doesn't work he becomes more violent because he hates himself for being vulnerable.

She'll eventually get a restraining order on him; he in turn won't pay any attention to it. If she's lucky he will go to jail for continuing to harass her. Then once he's in jail his right state of mind will return, and he'll wonder why he went to the extremes that he did. Not understanding that **Spiritual Warfare** took place. Not understanding that he was being manipulated by the devil.

On the other hand, if he has good sense, he will let her get on with her life, and realize that he can't make her love him through violence. If he doesn't have good sense, and is not caught by the police in time, the ultimate might happen.

Men who seek revenge on a woman will beat her unrecognizable. He will cut up her face with a knife, pour gasoline on her and light a match to her. He will splash her in the face with acid, shoot her in the face with a gun, or set her house on fire, with her in it. He is driven by the evil one to destroy her beauty so that no one else wants her. In some circumstances the man who seeks revenge initiates the ultimate pay back. He kills her. Sometimes he's driven by the evil one to also kill the children, the dog, and then himself. Therefore the evil one has accomplished his goal by destroying multiple lives.

Revenge doesn't stop at relationships. There is revenge between siblings, co workers seek revenge, friends, neighbor's, gang bangers, politicians, and the list goes on and on.

<u>Men categorized as Dogs</u>

Women wonder why so many men are what they consider Dogs. In most cases men become dogs due to being hurt and deceived by a woman whom they were madly in love with at an early age. And in turn want to hurt every woman that they come in contact with, feeling that all women are rotten whores that can't be trusted. Some men were hurt, abused, and disappointed by their mothers. Therefore grow up hating women and having no desire to ever love or respect a woman.

Some men were taught at an early age by older men who were hurt by women, that treating women disrespectful makes them **Hip, Slick and Cool.** Youngsters are being taught that the worse you treat a woman the better she will treat you. Sadly, in many circumstances this is true. As in situations where the woman has low self esteem and feels like she's not worthy of being respected or loved.

Youngsters of today are taught to believe that treating a woman with respect makes them soft. They are taught that being in a relationship with one girl is lame, that kissing isn't necessary. There is no use for romance in the lives of today's youths. The evil one has blinded them into not showing emotions. The young men of today feel that it is not masculine to be kind, gentle, and loving; they feel it's a sign of weakness. They are in the realms of **Spiritual Warfare,** and don't even know that it exists.

Take Control of Your Life

Life is like having two dogs inside of you. One is gentle and one is mean. Whichever one you feed the most is the one you'll become. One survives and the other you will starve to death. So always remember: feed the one of peace, and starve the one of anger to death.

You will struggle with **Spiritual Warfare** throughout life, good versus evil, right versus wrong. What you have to remember is that all goodness comes from **God** , and anything evil comes from the devil.

Take control of your lives. Open up your heart to **God,** through **Jesus Christ**. Therefore don't allow anger to disrupt your life. Don't allow the evil one to manipulate your mind into believing that living a foul life is **Hip, Slick and Cool**.

The devil can only do what you allow him to do. Trust and have faith in **God**. For **God** is love. Repent your sins to him, and **God,** through **Jesus Christ**, will give you peace of mind. **Spiritual Warfare** is real. That's why **God** gave all his children "**free will**"; you have the choice to choose good over evil, life over death. Choose your path wisely.

STORY 3

SPIRITUAL WARFARE/BEHIND BARS

The fight against **Spiritual Warfare,** and the desire of being **Hip, Slick and Cool** has caused many people to end up behind bars. Most people are incarcerated because they don't think or care about the consequences that go along with breaking the law. Many people end up behind bars because they will go to any extent, by any means necessary, right or wrong, trying to fill that void in their heart, that emptiness inside their soul.

Unfortunately most people believe the only way the void can be filled is by using drugs, drinking, gambling, shopping, paying for sex, etc. In order to indulge in these activities you must have money. So people rob, steal, lie, cheat, hustle, turn tricks and commit murder, whatever it takes, in order to get it. They believe that the love of money, the root of all evil, will solve all of their problems. So they try to fill that void by living in the fast lane, which eventually lands them in a penitentiary cell or in an early grave.

God created man and also created laws to be enforced in our lives to make it possible to keep order in the world. If we didn't have enforced laws the world would be off the hook. Unfortunately all over the world the ones who control the laws, paint a picture which is an illusion that keeps certain individuals in the dark. The illusion is set to make you believe that certain races of people are criminals and certain races of people aren't. You must recognize that all people are the same. We are all under one universal race. All of God's children have a choice of behaving **God**-like or behaving evil, which is the concept of **Spiritual Warfare**. No one is excluded from it.

<u>Juvenile Hall</u>

Many young men and women are set up to fail in life due to receiving the wrong information because they were taught at an early age that their lives are meaningless through the media, music, videos, etc. This is why they are victims of a life which consists of going back and forth to jail, due to their lifestyle of living in poverty, no father figure in the home, no education, drug abuse, emotional, mental, and physical abuse, which leads to self hate, low self esteem and no self worth.

Many of these unfortunate mislead children end up going to juvenile hall at an early age. Some after their first encounter hate the idea of being confined in the system, therefore get scared straight. Which helps them to turn their lives around so that they won't have to go back to juvenile hall again. Some may get raped or beat up during their first encounter of juvenile hall, and end up emotionally handicapped for the rest of their life. Others feel going to juvenile hall for the first time makes them a big shot, which gives them an oar of being **Hip, Slick and Cool.** They think nothing of it, that it's no big thing. Because they are young, they don't look at the big picture. They are not aware that they are experiencing the concept of **Spiritual Warfare.** The evil spirit ruining their lives.

Usually the first time these youngsters get busted, there parents are called and informed of the child's arrest and are asked to pick them up. Being that they are young, at times they don't get in trouble for going to juvenile hall because their parents feel sorry for them. Since they don't get in trouble for whatever they have done, many of them continue to break the law time after time, until eventually going back and forth to juvenile hall becomes part of their lifestyle.

Some youngsters get away with breaking the law over and over again. Therefore the addiction of fast living kicks in, and every time they break the law they get an adrenalin rush, a feeling of power, a feeling of being indestructible.

And before they know it they are addicted to get rich quick schemes, and the bigger risks they take the slicker they believe they are. They develop the feeling of power, that now they can't get caught, and they believe that they are invincible. They become addicted to the fast lane, fast money, fast women/men, fancy cars, and the bling-bling. **Hip, Slick and Cool,** the good life, is what they believe they are living, when in truth it is all an illusion of grander. The fact of the matter is, they are being manipulated by the evil one who is leading them to a life in the penitentiary or to an early grave.

Unfortunately they don't even think of the consequences behind breaking the law. They don't realize that their social security number and name is being ruined at an early age. They don't realize that they are ruining their chance to live a normal life in society. They think nothing of it. It's just juvenile hall, I'm a minor, it's not real jail. I can handle a few weeks or a few months of this – it's easy. So this cycle continues until they become eighteen and are at the age where they can go to the county jail.

Now a day's society deals with juveniles in a different way. There is no more in and out of juvenile hall. There is low tolerance for children who continue to break the law. The government has come up with the three strikes and you're out law.

Three Strike Law

Juveniles of today must realize that the three strike law is in effect to take them completely out of the box. This law is designed to ruin young lives. It's made to make young men and women who make mistakes at an early age suffer the consequences when they become adults. The three strike law is designed for young boys and girls who get caught up in the lifestyle of being **Hip, Slick and Cool.**

Genocide comes in all shapes, forms, and fashions. Today the laws are geared for the younger generation. Can you imagine a 3 strike law for juveniles? No one on **Gods** earth is perfect; we all make mistakes in life, especially in our youth. We all must learn from our mistakes. Many children of today are violent at early ages and disrespectful towards their parents due to mental health issues. Many of these children are products of their parents using drugs and alcohol at the conception of their birth.

Many of their parents are or were at one time in their lives, gang bangers, so the children follow suit because they learn by example. But there are also those young men and women who are targeted by the law enforcement due to their nationality or because of the communities in which they live.

These unfortunate children become victims of the prison system with intent for them to spend the rest of their lives in jail, by being harassed at an early age and being set up for this racist 3 strike law. These laws are made not by accident but by design to lock our children up as soon as possible, for the rest of their lives.

The 3 strike law is designed for population control. Which means if they incarcerate our children while they are young, they may not be able to produce any children when they become adults, because after getting busted 3 times they may spend the rest of their natural lives behind bars. Society also wants to set them up at an early age for life in prison, in order to use up their strength and endurance while their young, by using them for slave labor so that private industry can prosper and get richer from the convenience of cheap labor. **Spiritual Warfare** is in affect from the birth to the death of our children.

The County Jail

When you go to the County Jail you know for a fact that you are being punished. Hopefully you committed a crime and are not there by default. There are many people in the jail systems who haven't committed crimes. The county jail is designed for punishment. It's a pit stop before you go to the penitentiary.

The county jail is always over crowded. There are 4 – 6 men sometimes more, housed in a cell fit for two men. You are locked in your cell for twenty four seven unless they feel like letting you go outside on the roof on Fridays, but there's no guarantee. You and you're cell mates both eat and go to the toilet in your cell. It is filthy and also rat and roach infested. The guards and deputies treat the inmates with no respect, and you receive no peace or justice. There is racism in your face on a daily basis, and you are subject to get beat to death by your roommate(s) or by the guards or deputies at any given time.

The only good thing about being in the county jail is that you can receive visits. But there is a catch to that. Your wife, girlfriend or family member usually waits at least 1 – 2 hours, if they are lucky, in order to see you for fifteen minutes. Fortunately the inmates are allowed visits from Thursday to Sunday.

The Penitentiary

Living your life behind the walls in the penitentiary is no joke. Penitentiary time is not designed like it was back in the day. Back in the day when you went to the pen you could educate yourself by going to school, and at times even achieve a college degree. You could also learn a trade which would land you a job when you got out of the penitentiary. There were also support systems to help you get on your feet in order for you to be able to live a normal life after you did your time.

Now it's three strikes and you're out! If you get in trouble twice and go back to jail, you may never get out again. Young men and women eighteen, nineteen years old, who never even had a real girl friend or boy friend, have never been married, will never attend another family gathering. Some will never father or mother a child. Or if they have children, they will never see the outside world, and never again spend quality time with their children. Life wasted behind bars, where they may never get out again.

When certain classes of people are being set up to spend their lives in the penitentiary, it's a concept of **Spiritual Warfare**. You must realize that the powers at be, who are behind those curtains, camouflaged so that you cannot see them, are the law makers of this country and criminals themselves. Their jobs are to incarcerate as many poor people as possible. Especially certain races of people, in order to control the population. Minorities are mainly incarcerated in the County jail system and the Department of Corrections system. When the time comes and they are transferred to the Penitentiary, the law enforcement uses prisoners to work for slave wages in order to keep big business prosperous.

Spiritual Warfare, life gone down the drain behind senseless crimes like robbery, due to being hooked on narcotics, or robbery, due to being hooked on the greed of money. Or by getting busted for committing get rich quick schemes, or being caught with a pistol, carrying it around for kicks because of the power it has in your hand, making you feel invincible. All illusions from the evil one to make you feel **Hip, Slick and Cool**. When you live your life behind bars it is not worth 10 cents. A life behind bars is **Spiritual Warfare** at its worst. Penitentiary life equals Satan's Domain.

<u>My Husbands Story</u>

Young men and women I suggest that you turn your lives around before you waist it behind bars. Realize that going in and out of jail is no joke. Take it from me, I know. Been there, done that. But by the grace of **God**, I am here to talk about it. To tell you how **God** intervened and blessed me to make it out alive to tell my story of being **Hip, Slick and Cool**.

You see, I was raised with low self esteem, no self worth. When I was coming up I couldn't read and couldn't write. While attending school my classmates laughed at me when it came my turn to read, so I was afraid to go to class. Eventually, one day my truant officer came over to my house and told my mother that I hadn't been to school for so long that it was a shame. Yes I got a whopping, but the pain from the extension cord was nothing compared to the pain I received in that classroom.

Those young kids laughing at me made the enemy attack me at an early age with low self esteem, and no self worth. So I said to myself, I know what I'll do. I'll be the best hustler, I'll be the best pimp, I'll be the best con man, I'll be the best at anything that was **Hip, Slick and Cool**. But what It got me was a life in and out of prison, with memories of birthdays being passed up, and loved ones passing on while I was away. I did not realize that all the time I was going in and out of prison; that my name was becoming fouler and fouler in the system. I was now labeled as a convict and an ex-felon.

Life Behind Bars

The things that take place behind those penitentiary walls are **Spiritual Warfare** at its worst. I'm not a racist man; I wasn't brought up that way, but being racist runs deep in the penitentiary. This race hates that race; all races hate the black race. You can't do this with this race; you can't do that with that race. The sad truth is, all races want to have the power to control the penitentiary.

Who's going to run the penitentiary? The battle begins and never seems to end. A person from one race sticks you with a knife, you stick one of theirs, they stick ten of yours. A riot breaks out and the gun man's shooting at the crowd. So you think, when all the time he might be shooting at a certain race of people that he hates because of the color of their skin, rather than the person with a weapon. You never really know. **Spiritual Warfare**, at its worst behind those walls.

You must realize that living your life in and out of prison is not **Hip, Slick and Cool**. The truth of the matter is that a lot of youngsters think it is because their brother went to prison and made it out, so sub consciously there not afraid to follow his footsteps. Or your mother went to prison, your aunties, and your uncles, your big homies all went, so it don't mean nothing when they bust you. In your mind you feel that since your homies are in prison they'll look out for you.

You must realize that **Spiritual Warfare** is out to get you. The evil one doesn't want you to reach your potential and become a doctor, lawyer, scientist, teacher, or whatever you are designed to be in life. **Hip, Slick and Cool** has taken you off of your course, and now you are an X convict.

Behind those walls is an everyday struggle. When you wake up and the doors unlock for you to go out onto the yard, you don't know if it's your day to get stabbed or if it's your day to break something into someone else. You also don't know if it's your day to be accidentally or purposely shot, when you haven't bothered anybody or done anything to anyone.

If you're lucky enough not be killed in prison, and even more lucky not to come out with stab wounds or gunshot wounds, you'll come out with ulcers from worrying half to death about what you had to deal with on a daily basis. But you deal, while time continues to go by – days, weeks, months, years.

The amount of time people are given now days is ridiculous. The system sets the bail amount for hundreds of thousands of dollars for small crimes such as: people having a narcotic problem, people robbing other people due to having a narcotic problem, people dealing drugs in order to support their narcotic problem. The laws are set up to make sure poor people cannot afford to be bailed out. The bail amount is so high at times; you'd think the suspect had shot the president.

Drug business is also big business in America. Where do the drugs come from? Poor people do not grow cocaine in their back yards. Realize that certain races of people are targeted when it comes to being busted for narcotics. Certain races of people will receive more time than other races of people. This cycle is never ending. You will receive more time for rock cocaine than powder cocaine. And that's because the cocaine is distributed in powder form to the poor man who then turns it into rock form.

In many instances men and women get locked up because their mates are materialistic, and the habit of having material possessions drives people into committing crimes. Remember: Kings and Queens go together like witches and warlocks. Choose a mate that is designed for you, someone that you can be together with in order to live life on a positive tip. Don't choose the fast life; don't choose someone who wants to live in the fast lane. You will only get involved in criminal activity by trying to live above your means, which leads to breaking the law in order to possess fast money.

This way of living will only turn your life upside down and have you end up in an early grave or in prison for the rest of your life. Wondering how you got there. Looking out of your cell window at night. Crying in your pillow because now you've gotten 25 or 35 to life for burglary or robbery due to stealing from someone in order to conceive money quickly. Robbery and burglary leads to gun play or murder at times, which leads to receiving sentences like 250 years plus life. Never going home again, behind the blind leading the blind. **Spiritual Warfare** at its worst.

Fast Money – Fast Living

Many youngsters get influenced into selling drugs because they can't find a job that pays big money. Many of them haven't graduated from high school. They haven't gone to school to learn a trade or college to hopefully become successful. They don't understand that they have to crawl before they walk. They are made to believe that working at MacDonald's or Burger King is an insult, those kinds of jobs are for chumps. They want big money and they want it quickly. They don't believe in living their lives as an honest working person.

So somebody puts a dope sack in their hand and tells them that they can come up by dealing drugs. They don't see this person as they really are, because these youngsters are under the illusion of **Hip, Slick and Cool.** Remember "Just because you see my teeth, don't mean I'm smiling at you". Someone who sets you up to deal drugs is not looking out for your best interest. Dealing and using drugs is a concept of **Spiritual Warfare.** The devil planting illusions in your mind by feeding it negative information, but making you believe that it's positive.

So you start selling drugs. You feel like a big shot because you're making big money quickly. You are up, and therefore can purchase an abundance of material possessions. You're on top of the world. Is receiving this money a gift from **God**? Do you believe **God** gave you this blessing of having fast money? Is selling poison to unfortunate people something **God** would have you do? Is having men and women kill, steal, sell their bodies, and abandon their families to purchase these drugs, something **God** would want?

You must realize that if a blessing doesn't come from our Father, that it comes from Satan. Realize that if you don't work for **God,** that you work for the devil. Nothing good will come to you from dealing drugs. You will have no peace of mind and you constantly have to watch your back. The money comes easy, but it leaves as easy as it comes. And sooner or later you will pay for those ill gotten gains. Sooner or later you will end up in prison for dealing drugs or you will end up six feet below ground level due to the consequences of drug dealing.

The jail system is full of young men and women whose talents and potentials were wasted away due to one mistake. One mistake and there never getting out of jail. In many instances youngsters go to jail due to being put up to do a crime because they were part of a gang. After they get busted they feel safe going to jail, because they know the jail system is full of their homies.

On your first encounter in prison gang members know for a fact that you just came through. They realize that you are new at the jail game, so they give you the jail initiation. Just like on the street they put you through the test. Which is more than likely a violent crime. A common way to prove yourself in jail is to stab or kill another person. If you accomplish your test, you're in with the homies. Then you end up lost in the system forever. Satan playing you out of pocket, and you can't even see it because you think your being **Hip, Slick and Cool. Spiritual Warfare**, evil at its worst.

You're on your own

When someone first gets busted a friend or two might acknowledge their incarceration. But after a short period of time, depending on how much time they have, nobody will care about them except mothers, true lovers, and maybe their family members. Their so called homies may be in their corner at first, and send them a money order, a postal stamped envelope, and maybe once in a while pay for a food package. But after they have been missing off the block and out of action for a certain length of time, their homies will talk about them for a minute, but as time passes by, their name will just fade away. Eventually they will be lost, out of sight, out of mind, behind those bars for however long, maybe the rest of their lives, from trying to be **Hip, Slick and Cool.**

Population Control

We must realize that foul living, murder and mayhem, which we face on a daily basis in this dark world, is perpetrated by our society. Not by accident but by design. We must recognize that there are certain races of people who can produce as many children as they choose, and other races of people who cannot produce many or even any at all without the help of fertility drugs.

Yes we are in the concept of **Spiritual Warfare** - Population Control - Where certain races of people are being purposely targeted into being incarcerated at an early age so that they cannot produce children. **Spiritual Warfare** - Population Control – Society targets certain communities where it is designed to lock children up as soon as possible, before their child baring years. Incarcerating these young men during puberty. Knowing in many instances that they end up having sex with men in prison. Therefore becoming gay or contracting HIV and spreading it to young girls when or if they return home from prison. At the same time incarcerating young women who in many instances become lesbians and aren't interested in becoming mothers.

Spiritual Warfare – Population Control – Society targets these certain races of people to prevent them from achieving greatness in life. Making them believe that they are inferior, destined to becoming drug dealers, pimps, hustlers, women abusers, whores, **Hip, Slick and Cool.** Instead of doctors, lawyers, engineers, scientists, teachers, and people of high status.

Who's behind it all? An unseen enemy who plays all kinds of games in order to trick you out of your life, into an early grave. And if he can't trick you into an early grave, he'll trick you into a life behind prison bars. And once he gets you behind prison bars, your name is not Mr. Smith or Miss Smith, it becomes C55555 or B66666 or D77777. Whatever your CDC number is, that's who you are. You are no longer considered a human being, you are just a number.

There are also industries, companies and private owners who own stock in the County Department of Corrections. Commodity for the jail system is another form of slavery. Realize that when you go in front of those judges, they see dollar signs by locking you up. The police department is so corrupt these days that they do whatever they want because they have the power to. They arrest people knowing that the offense won't hold. But just wanting to inconvenience you by maybe making you lose your job, or your apartment, or hoping you have some other offense which will keep you in jail.

<u>Three Strikes and Your Out</u>

Spiritual Warfare; just because men have a penis between their legs, doesn't make them a man. Man is mind; we must understand that **God** comes first. We must realize that if we keep **God** on our minds, in our hearts, and in our homes, everything positive will fall in place. If we follow **God**, **God** will lead us in the right direction.

Spiritual Warfare; the enemy will have you behind bars in a wink of an eye from trying to be **Hip, Slick and Cool.** This is the design of the enemy: If you've done a crime in the past as a juvenile, then commit another crime when you're a young man, and one more as an adult. Then decide to do good, clean up your life and become a good citizen. But you slip and make one more bad move. Before you know it your bail is a million dollars plus, behind making another mistake in life.

Past records and strikes are designed for people who live in poverty, people who feel their only way of survival is a life of crime. So they choose being **Hip, Slick and Cool** to survive. The **Hip Slick and Cool** way of life is their only strategy. This is the life set up for them by Society. Not by accident, but by design. Society intentionally makes it hard on these individuals. Society intentionally makes it hard for them to survive. Hard for them to get a decent job. Hard for them to stay out of trouble from being harassed by the police at an early age. Hard for them to attend college. Hard for them to take care of themselves. Hard on them to produce, let alone support a family. So three strikes and you're out,

THREE STRIKES AND YOU'RE OUT!!!!!

<u>Straighten Up and Fly Right</u>

Prison life ain't no joke. I suggest you straighten up, fly right, and understand that there is only one way to live your life, and that is the right way. Live your life the way **God** designed you to live it. He didn't design you to end up going to prison behind dealing drugs, using drugs, pimping and conning prostitutes, hustling, get rich quick schemes, counter fit money, greed, wanting material items that you don't need, or wanting possessions someone else has. Whatever you desire in life you must work hard for it. It feels better when you earn it and you'll appreciate it more.

Please recognize that the only way to make it in life is through the power of faith, along with hard work, being humble, praying, studying, and knowing the word of **God.** Therefore you must accept **Jesus Christ** as your **Lord and Savior.** Work on working hard. Work on reaching your potential. Pray that **God** show you what your purpose in life is. Know that you don't have to live a life of foulness. Know that you can choose what team to be on, **God's** team or Satan's team.

Realize that you are a child of **God**. Realize that you are a part of **God**. Know that you possess the power of **God,** and can do anything your heart desires through **Jesus Christ**. Recognize **Spiritual Warfare,** a struggle we all face in life. Choose the spirit of the light, for that is the spirit of **God**. **God** gave us all **free will**, use it wisely. Only good can come from **God's** desires. **God's** desire is that we love one another, be kind, patient, gentle, humble, compassionate, and generous.

STORY 4

SPIRITUAL WARFARE/FAMILY VALUES

As far back as Adam and Eve, we as human beings were blessed by **God** with **"Free Will"**. **God** blessed all of his children with the freedom of choosing to live our lives by both reading and practicing his word, or to live our lives grasping for worldly desires.

<u>Family Values</u>

God's plan for us (as a family unit) is that we (as man and woman) marry, be fruitful, and bare children, in order to keep the human race abundant. **God's** plan for a man and woman is to love him, love one another, obey your marriage vows, and keep the family united.

Being rewarded with someone who truly loves you is a gift from **God**; therefore it is our responsibility to fight **Spiritual Warfare**, which is a constant battle between good and evil. The only solution in upholding a solid marriage, as well as the family unit, is by keeping **God** first and foremost in your lives. For if you don't, the union between the two is destined to fail.

The Devils job is to oppose whatever **God** wants. Satan will use as many evil acts as possible in order to cause conflict within the family unit. His job is to destroy the family, or if possible, destroy a happy relationship between a man and woman before it becomes solid enough for marriage. The evil one will try to tear the family apart by any means necessary.

The father is the Engineer of the family. If he is on track the whole family is on track. If the enemy can run the father away from the home, he weakens the family, and the children are left to figure out their role in this world on their own. The mother can only do what she is designed to do, and the enemy is aware of that.

If the family unit is not filled with the spirit of **Jesus Christ**, the evil one will try every trick in the book to run the father away from the household. The devil will convince the father that he is not worthy of employment, and therefore unable to fend for the family. He will convince the father that he is worthless and weak. Which will drive the father into developing the mind frame of **Hip, Slick and Cool**.

Spiritual Warfare - The husband will develop low self esteem, no self worth, and will therefore start conjuring up get rich quick schemes. He will then start drinking, using drugs, going to strip clubs, turning tricks with prostitutes, and self medicating himself, in order to ease his pain. Then the arguing and fighting amongst the family begins, which more than likely leads to the father ending up in jail or moving out of the household, therefore abandoning the family.

The devil will in turn begin to play on the mother's thoughts; manipulating her mind into believing that her husband is cheating on her. Satan will tempt the husband with fast women in order for him to be swayed into cheating. The evil one will sway the mother of the house into dressing sexy in order for her to attract other men, causing her to eventually cheat also. Satan will drive a couple who were once in love, into hating one another. The evil one plays on your mind. If you don't have the spirit of **God** to fight off his temptations you are lost.

<u>The Male Child</u>

If a male child is raised by both parents he learns the values of being in a relationship and usually marries himself. If he is fortunate enough to be in a family which lives by the word of **God**, he sees how a woman should be treated by the way his father treats his mother, and therefore learns to respect women. He also learns how a man should be treated, nurtured and loved by a woman; by the way his mother treats his father. Children are taught by example.

On the other hand, if a boy child is raised by both parents and the parents are not practicing **God's** word, they are more than likely in a relationship that is off the hook, and in the struggle of **Spiritual Warfare**. He is more than likely in a home where the mother and father argue, fight, disrespect each other, use foul language, use drugs and alcohol, and are unhappy most of the time. He too will most likely be in a relationship or marriage where there is no respect, harmony or peace of mind.

All couples argue and have disagreements. But if you're filled with the spirit of **Jesus Christ,** you know how to forgive and therefore an argument will fizzle out quickly. But if you're filled with the spirit of the devil, arguments can lead into disaster.

When a male child is brought up in a single parent household run by the mother or father, and they live by the word of **God,** the child has a chance to become a responsible person. That's if the word of **God** is a large part of his growing up.

When a male child is brought up in a single parent household run by the mother, has no father figure, and the mother is not practicing **God's** word. The boy child has to figure out on his own "What it takes to be a man", and "What his role is in the family". He considers himself the man of the house when he doesn't have a clue what the role of a man consists of.

So he goes out into the world to find out on his own what it takes to become a man. The wrong information takes its toll. The information he receives from the world is evil, **Hip, Slick and Cool**. By the age of 11 or 12 he starts running with the wrong crowd or ends up joining a gang. He learns how to speak with a foul mouth. He starts smoking cigarettes and drinking alcohol, which leads to weed and maybe crack or meth.

Eventually he becomes a dope dealer. Believing in his mind that this is the good life. He longs to have as many girlfriends as possible. Which leads to numerous babies' mamas and/or sexually contracted diseases. He will have a child here and a child there, not being a father to any of them. The mother in many cases is a child herself, which amounts to a child raising a child. In some cases she is also a product of a single parent household. And the cycle goes on and on.

The Female Child

When a female child is raised in a family by both parents she too learns the value of being in a relationship and will most likely get married herself. If she is fortunate enough to be raised in a family that lives by the word of **God**, she will see firsthand how a woman should be treated, and will know how to treat her man with respect and love. As stated: Children learn by example.

When a female child is raised in a family by both parents who are not practicing **God's** word, she will experience unhappiness, lack of love, lack of trust, lack of respect, fighting, arguing, child abuse, drug abuse, foul language, and every other act of foulness the devil can conger up. She will more than likely not do well in relationships because she will not expect men to respect her. Because her mother was not respected by her father, nor her father by her mother, she in turn will not respect her men either.

When a female child is brought up in a single household run by her mother or her father, and they are practicing and living by the word of **God**. She has the chance to become a responsible young lady, if the word of **God** is a large part of her growing up.

When a female child is brought up in a single parent household run by her mother and there is no father figure. She grows up looking for love in all the wrong places. In many cases she will hook up with an older man because she is searching for a father figure. In some cases the young female ends up with the wrong older man, who will influence her into turning tricks and/or abusing drugs. Convincing her that it's **Hip, Slick and Cool** to do so. Or she will have a baby by the first man who tells her that he loves her. This cycle may continue until she has four or five children by different daddies before she reaches the age of 25.

She more than likely will also have abandonment issues. Due to the absence of her father it will be hard for her to put her trust in men. She will always be under the suspicion that her man is cheating and will abandon her. She will not believe she is good enough. She will believe that she is not worthy of being loved. More than likely she will have low self esteem. All elements designed by the evil one to destroy lives.

Trust in God

God's word is designed for us to recognize how to live life and how to be conscience of the light within us, which is the **Holy Spirit**. You must follow the light by listening to your heart, where **God** lies. The light brings joy, happiness, sincerity, peace, and all other good feelings into your soul.

Remember – If it's not a good feeling, than it doesn't belong to **God.** Therefore if you follow your heart and read and live by **God's** word, you will understand how to live your life in peace and harmony. Be aware that in the end, there is a final grade that you must pass in the school of life.

You must fight the forces of evil, which are the forces of darkness in this world. If you are a husband and father, be the spiritual leader of your family. Keep **God** first and foremost. If you are a man who is not married and you have children. Take care of your children. Children are gifts from **God.**

No matter what tricks the enemy tries in order to pull you away from your family, don't bite. Communication with your Queen and children is the key. Be the king of your castle. The father is the voice which says "Let's go to Church", "Let's get prepared to pray for the food we are about to receive". The father sets the standards and the guidelines. Follow **Gods** word and your family will follow you. The female will follow the male and the children will follow him as well. **Trust in God!**

STORY 5

SPIRITUAL WARFARE/GAMBLING

Gambling addiction, as most addictions, usually begins when a person reaches their adolescent years. Many teenagers start off by shooting craps or playing card games. At first gambling is fun to them, they look at it as something to do to pass the time away. There is no pressure involved. You win some, you lose some. Satan manipulates your mind into believing that gambling will not become an obsession or an addiction.

Eventually the obsession sets in. But you're in denial. You don't realize that the forces of evil are slowly drawing you in. You don't realize that the devil is manipulating your mind into making you believe that gambling your money away makes you **Hip, Slick and Cool.** You feel, "I just like to gamble". "It's fun and exciting". When all the time your being sucked into a life of lies, deceit, havoc, and emotional abuse. You've entered into the battle of **Spiritual Warfare,** good versus evil, right versus wrong.

In most instances the gambler starts off gambling small sums of money. They may start of by buying one lotto ticket per week. Then in some cases, it escalates to five lotto tickets per week. Even though the odds are a million to one per ticket, the gambler feels they have a chance to win and therefore develops the habit of buying lotto tickets as part of their weekly expense. Some people are what you call functional gamblers and only develop the obsession of buying lotto tickets or maybe going to Las Vegas two to three times per year.

On the other hand you have the hard core gamblers who bet on sports, such as; basketball games, baseball games, hockey, boxing, golf, and so on.

There are also Pool sharks and card hustlers. But it doesn't stop there. A gambler will bet on anything, such as; horse races, dog races, or a roach racing, if they can get someone to bet against them.

The Addiction becomes bigger and bigger

As you continue to gamble, your gambling desire increases. In other words, you're hooked. Just like any other addiction you want to gamble more and more. Just like any other addiction you're trying to fill that hole inside of you, that void that you cannot seem to fill. Satan, the unseen enemy, has you in his grips, and you are not aware of it.

After continuous years of gambling the gambler knows it's a problem, but can't stay away from it. They haven't a clue that it's all due to **Spiritual Warfare**. Eventually the evil spirit takes its toll, manipulating your mind until all your thoughts are consumed with gambling. When you're awake all you think about is making a bet. When you're asleep you dream about gambling.

Do you gamble to win? Do you gamble to lose? Why do you continue to gamble? Why can't you stop? What drives you to continue? Is it that you are hoping to win large sums of money? Or is it the thrill of getting close to winning, but never actually winning?

Under the Illusion of the Evil Spirit

The evil spirit drives you to gamble. You are under the illusion of the devil who manipulates your mind into making you believe that gambling is **Hip, Slick and Cool.** The evil one who whispers in your ear saying things like: Next time you'll win big, keep on trying, you can't win if you don't try, you can't stop now, you need another fix. So the harder you try to stop, the stronger the evil one drives you to continue.

You must realize that the enemy attacks the mind and tells you that you're going to win. It tells you to just keep on betting. Gambling gives you an adrenalin rush. You actually feel high while you're gambling. You feel as if you have the art down to a science when you're winning. You feel like you are in control. But in reality you're in Spiritual trouble. You don't know it and can't see it because you're in an illusion, playing in the boxing ring with the enemy. But you can't win, you can't knock him out, you can't defeat the devil. He'll toy with you and toy with you. Only to drive you deeper and deeper in debt. Eventually one addiction leads to another addiction. You start drinking and smoking heavy to sooth your nerves. One habit leads to another habit.

At times you will win large sums of money, but in turn gamble it all away to win more. Then you run out of money, emptying your bank account, and you become dispirit to get more. So you pawn your car, and when that money runs out you pawn your home and anything else of value that you have. Therefore giving up your lively hood. Now your even more dispirit and have nowhere else to turn. So you borrow money from loan sharks or big time drug dealers. After you gamble that money away where do you go? You're backed against a wall, between a rock and a hard place. There is no way out. In these circumstances either you get beat to death by the low life's you borrowed from, or you take your own life. Satan has therefore done what he does, he manipulates, deceives and destroys.

Gambling addition leads to broken homes and abandonment of your family and friends. Eventually, like any other junkie, you'll sell your body for money to gamble. When in reality you're selling your soul to the devil. A gambling addiction is like holding a carrot in front of a donkey; you keep chasing the carrot, trying to get a bite.

Then there are people who are extremely wealthy who feel that they have money to burn and feel as if they can throw it away on gambling. Or you have people with good paying jobs who choose to take on the habit of gambling because they feel as if they can afford to. If these people are compulsive, they too may develop a strong appetite for gambling.

When working people develop the habit of gambling and the obsession sets in, they start missing work because they have stayed up all night. And before they know it they have run through all of their money. Being that they are used to having money, they go through any means necessary to get more. This is when embezzlement comes into play. A person who was once responsible is now a thief, liar and deceiver. Satan has conquered another soul. They are in the grips of **Spiritual Warfare.** Eventually their greed winds them in jail, wondering what happened to turn their lives upside down.

Many have tried support groups like Gamblers Anonymous. They may help you, they may not. Sometimes you feel as if you are cured, but it's just the enemy giving you a break for a minute. Then before you know it the devil is back in your head, manipulating your mind, saying things like; go gamble one more time, you can win now. When in reality you know in your gut that you cannot win. You are in an ongoing cycle that can only be stopped by turning your life over to **God**, through **Jesus Christ**.

Professional Gamblers
-

There are people who are considered professional gamblers. People who gamble for a living. In many instances they make a good living. In some cases they have a skill. But in most circumstances they are what you would consider professional cheaters. Satan allows them to win thousands and thousands of dollars. They buy big houses and fancy cars. They live the life of a big shot. They develop the mind set of being **Hip, Slick and Cool.** Believing they are in control of their gambling and cheating habit. When they too are in an illusion set by the evil one, with their minds being manipulated to believe that they are lucky, fortunate and therefore cannot loose or be found out.

So they go on cheating because there good at it. Then, as he always does, Satan shows up with his calculated moves. He uncovers the tricks of this professional cheater. He shows their fellow gamblers what he/she is really about. The cheater is then put on Front Street and is exposed of their flym-flaming ways. What do they do now? How can they get out of the mess that they have created?

The word gets out to fellow gamblers about their deception. They now have people looking for them. They have to run and hide to escape big time gamblers whom they have beatin' out of their money. Who in turn hire hit people to eliminate them. Sooner or later they will be found, and when they are, it will be the end of their demise.

Messing with people's money is no joke. When they are finally found, their last day on earth can be handled in many ways. Either they will be shot to death, beat to death, hands cut off for cheating and left to bleed to death, throat cut, body left in a car to be driven off of a cliff, smothered to death, or set on fire while still alive.

You must realize that if a blessing doesn't come from **God**, it comes from the devil. Realize that there is a difference between the two. **Spiritual Warfare** is real. If you are doing evil, you are being driven by evil forces. Only good comes from the forces of **God, our Father** through **Jesus Christ.**

God Through Jesus Christ Is The Only Way Out
-

The only way out of your gambling addiction is to seek **God's** mercy through **Jesus Christ**. All addictions are foul and come from the devil;

therefore you alone cannot break the chain on them. Our temple, which is our body, is like a house or a vessel that someone rents out. Either the **Spirit of God** will dwell in your temple, or the enemy will dwell in it.

God gave us all "free will". Which means you have the power to choose good over evil. The devil only does what you allow him do. So you must fill that emptiness you feel inside, that void that you are trying to fill with gambling, fill it with the spirit of **Jesus,** which is the **Holy Spirit**. If you choose **Jesus** you will be blessed with peace of mind.

God can remove the desire of any addiction. Trust in him; turn your life over to him. Repent your sins and remove the enemy's power over you. Let **God,** through the spirit of **Jesus,** enter into your heart. **Jesus** is the way the truth and the life.

STORY 6

SPIRITUAL WARFARE/GANG BANGIN'

There have been gangs in our society since the beginning of civilization. Way back in time, tribes would fight against other tribes for ownership of territories. Now a day's gangs fight amongst each other for drug territories. Yes, gang bangin has been around for a long time. Today, it is way out of control.

I remember back in the day when gangs would fist fight to see who the baddest dude in the neighborhood was, or who the baddest dude in school was. After the fight was over, there might be a black eye or busted lip amongst the fighters. Every now and then someone would get cut or stabbed with a knife and would have to go to the hospital to get stitches. Or maybe someone might get busted in the head with a brick and have to ice down a hickie. Sometimes the entire gangs would fist fight each other. Violence is never good, but it was very seldom that someone died back in the day, behind a gang fight.

Today gang members take the easy way out. They all carry guns and sneak around shooting each other, as well as innocent people. Killing each other due to a particular color someone has on, or for no reason at all. Many innocent youngsters have been mistaken or assumed of being gang bangers because of their dress code of baggy pants hanging below their waists.

While conducting initiations, gang bangers shoot into crowds of people for the purpose of killing an innocent person. They also initiate drive by shootings, and at times when aiming at a rival gang banger, shoot innocent people by mistake. It might be a baby riding a bicycle, or a person walking down the street, or they may shoot a bullet through someone's window or wall.

Then you have gang members that kill people due to hatred and racism. Children who are taught at a young age that their race is superior, therefore no one else deserves to live an abundant life on this earth except their race of people. Or gang bangers that become racist while incarcerated, and bring their hatred onto the outside world. It doesn't matter what color or gender you are when it comes to gang bangin. All nationalities of people do it, White, Black, Asian, Hispanics, males and females. All nationalities kill their own people, in many cases. It is a senseless form of genocide, evil at its worst.

The sad thing about gang bangin is that these kids feel it's **Hip, Slick, and Cool** to do so. They don't realize that they are being manipulated by the devil to live the life of a murder, robber, thief, drug dealer, hustler or pimp. While being disrespectful to their total environment, be it their mother, father, siblings, and anyone else they encounter with. They don't look at the big picture of where gang bangin will lead them, which is either time in jail or to an early grave.

There are so many children who are smart and have talents beyond measure, but never get to reach their potential because of being short changed by gang bangin. Due to this fast paced world that we live in, our children are under the illusion, set by the evil one, to make them believe that living foul, making quick money, and having an abundance of material possessions, makes them **Hip, Slick and Cool.**

The young men of today also believe that they can never have too many girl friends. So they disrespect them all, and don't believe in having a loving one on one relationship.

Why do people gang bang?

In some instances children gang bang in order to fit in with what other children do. They feel it is **Hip, Slick and Cool** to gang bang because it gives them a false sense of power. Many children are followers, and therefore fall in with the wrong crowd. Some children receive no guidance or direction at home. So they join gangs believing they will get schooled, only to receive negative information and guidance.

In some cases children have low self esteem or no education. Some children have no father figure to look up to and admire. Then there are children who join gangs because big duck leads little duck. Meaning their big brother is in a gang so they follow suit. At times gang members follow suite of gang bangin from generation to generation; grandfather, father, son, and on down the line. Some youngsters feel it's just the right thing to do.

On many occasions when children reach 9 through 12 years of age, older children, 14 through 16, bully them into gang bangin. The older children pressure the younger children to join their gangs by intimidation, which makes them eventually join. Some children can't even go to school in peace, afraid if they don't join a gang that they will get jumped. Gang bangin, **Spiritual Warfare,** evil at its worst. Young men and women lost, with no hope in sight.

<u>The gang becomes your family</u>

When a child joins a gang, they are considered a family member to that gang. Therefore taking on an artificial love. They are made to believe that the home boys and home girls will die for them. New found bangers are made to believe that a home boy or girl will take a bullet for them. When in reality they have joined the forces of evil. Predators who prey on the young to do their dirty work; such as selling dope, stealing cars, robbing stores, robbing people, and any other foul act you can imagine.

While feeling this gang is their family, the child takes on a feeling of belonging, a feeling of being a part of something. These are your home boys and home girls, who in reality would sell you out for $2.00 if their backs were against a wall.

In your mind, you really believe that you are in charge of your neighborhood (the hood), that you are controlling things, because the evil one has manipulated your mind to make you feel you are dangerous, the tough guy who everyone fears. When in reality, like everyone else has to; you have to pay rent, spend money at your neighborhood store, and pay taxes. Which means you are not in charge or in control of anything or anyone. Gang bangin gives you a false sense of power, which is an illusion from the evil one. **God** is in charge and in control of every aspect in life.

The new found gang banger must also go through an initiation where they have to kill an innocent person, anyone they choose, in order to become fully fledged. Or they take a beating from around 10 gang bangers. If they come out of the beating acting hard, they move up in rank. If they cry like a baby, they try again. Once they become a full fledged gang banger they receive a name or title. They inherit an older bangers name, such as: Big

Dog/Little Dog, Crazy Dog/Little Crazy Dog, Wine-o/Little Wine-o, or Lefty/Little Lefty, etc.

The Older gang bangers teach the younger gang bangers what they know, which is nothing but foulness. How can they be teachers when they are lost themselves? They pass down negative information, the blind leading the blind. Wanna be gangsters, going nowhere, with no meaning or purpose in life. Foul living, the use of foul language, young men disrespecting young women, young women disrespecting each other, babies growing up with no fathers, young men and women going to the penitentiary, and useless deaths.

<u>Female Gang Bangin</u>

Sadly, there are more and more females joining gangs. Just as young men need a father figure in their lives, so do young females. There are so many families today that are single parented, so many families with the absence of the father. Young men need a father or father figure to show them how to be a responsible man. Young women need a father or father figure to show them how women should be respected and treated in life.

Many of the young females of today are living foul lives. They seem to have no respect for themselves or for each other. There is no loyalty among the young women of today, whether they are in gangs or not. They will share, or in turn take one of their homies boy friend's at the drop of a hat, while feeling no remorse. They disrespect their parents, and any other elder with whom they encounter with. Our youth is manipulated and driven by the evil one, and have no clue what's going on. No clue that they are under the concept of **Spiritual Warfare**, good versus evil.

Many young men are now being confronted, disrespected and harassed by female gang bangers. They talk to the young men as if they have on skirts, and the girls wear the pants, (saggin' pants at that). They are loud, unruly, angry, and are ready to fight at the drop of a hat. They have no hope in life. If you ask them why they are so full of violence, they tell you," my mother is", So, I am too. They are blinded into believing that living foul is **Hip, Slick and Cool.**

Even more sadly is the trend of gang bangin lesbians. There is a new trend of older lesbian women gang bangers, whose mission is to turn out as many young girls as possible into lesbianism along with gang bangin. This trend is steadily increasing due to the way of the world. This world that feeds our youth negative information. Information that is against the word of

God.

<u>Gang Dress Code</u>

Gang bangers have a dress code of tea shirts and baggy pants hanging below their behinds. The truth is, this design of clothing began in jail where the inmates did not have belts to hold their pants up, so they had no choice but to let their paints drop below their waistlines.

Sadly, the incarcerated homosexuals wear their paints below their behinds when they are advertising for a new boyfriend. This is to identify who they are, while making an easy access to the target area (if you know what I mean). Open up your eyes gang bangers, why would someone want their entire behind out except for one reason? There is nothing **Hip, Slick and Cool** about dressing this way. In reality it makes you look trifling with no respect for yourself.

What's even sadder is the fact that this style of dress is adapted by all youth as the trend of dressing. Our young men and women believe that saggin' paints makes them look **Hip, Slick and Cool.** Therefore youngsters who were never in gangs get mistaken for being in one because of the way they dress. There have been many instances where innocent young people have been shot, crippled for life or killed for following a trend of dress, for wanting to be in style, wanting to fit in.

<u>Wake Up</u>

Don't allow negate energy to make you give up in life. You must realize that there are evil forces that manipulate people's minds to do evil, which is the concept of **Spiritual Warfare.** Don't be a part of something that's going to destroy your life. Don't be a part of something that is designed by the devil to cut your life short. Don't be the cause of mothers and fathers weeping in their homes due to losing their child behind gang bangin. Be wise; don't make the mortuaries and flower shops rich behind your ignorance.

Stay in school. Education is so important in life. Learn and grasp at all the positive information that you can. Don't focus on fast money; get rich quick schemes, fast women/men, designer clothes/shoes and the bling-bling while you're still young. Allow yourself to grow up and earn an honest living. Then you can live a comfortable life.

Fast living will only have you ending up in prison or in an early grave. Take the slow approach in life. Be the tortoise, not the hare. Because in the long run the ones who live fast, die fast. It's OK to work at McDonalds or Burger King until you achieve your potentials in life. Strive for excellence.

The more you listen to your heart, the easier life will be. **God** is in your heart, **God** is love. Satan manipulates your mind. All evil desires and thoughts come from him.

You were created by **God.** You weren't created to gang bang. You weren't created to be in the negative environment of gang bangin. You weren't created to do drive buys, sell drugs and disrespect innocent people. You weren't created to be a killer. When you have these evil desires, you are being driven, manipulated by the evil one.

You must stand up against **Spiritual Warfare**, and fulfill your dreams. Be wise enough to stay away from negativity. Understand that evil is a negative energy that you don't have to be a part of. The enemy's job is to keep you ignorant to the real pleasures in life. Don't be afraid to say no to gang bangers. Keep **God** first in your life, and he will keep you out of harm's way. Understand that we all have an emptiness in our hearts, a void that needs to be filled in order for us to fill complete. Fill that void with the holy spirit of **God** through our **Lord** and **Savior Jesus Christ**.

<u>Trust in God</u>

Attending Church will give you a start of positive thinking. You will hear a message that will enter into your soul, which is your holy spirit. You will hear a message sent from **God** that can save your life, if you want to be saved. Faith comes from hearing the word of **God**. But first you must find the light from within yourself. You must develop a relationship with our father **God.** Reading the Bible is not always clear, so begin with small versus and escalate your reading. Go to Bible study and learn the word of **God**. Reading the word will give you peace of mind and comfort to deal with this dark world.

Remember: It is easier to put the light out from within yourself and join the darkness around you. Don't put out your light. Be who **God** designed you to be. Don't be a follower. Fulfill your dreams and reach your goals. Use the brain **God** blessed you with. Be a positive person. You are a child of **God,** which is why he gave you **free will**, the power to choose good over evil. The devil will only do what you allow him to do. Trust in **God**. Learn to love yourself and also love your fellow man. You are a part of **God,** and **God** is love. You have the choice, choose your path wisely.

STORY 7

SPIRITUAL WARFARE/GENERATION X

(Generation X, as in X'd Out)

Today's younger generation is tomorrow's future. What a scary thought to realize. Unfortunately, a considerable amount of today's younger generation are products of alcoholics, pill heads, meth heads, crack heads, sherm heads, acid heads and heroin addicts, and many of them were born into this world as addicts themselves. A majority of these children grew up in broken homes where one parent or both parents were not in their lives. Many had to grow up on their own and not only raise themselves, but also raise their brothers and sisters. Many of them have never experienced true happiness, and in turn don't believe they deserve any.

The younger generation is under an illusion that living foul, using foul language, abusing drugs, disrespecting others and raising their children to do the same, is **Hip, Slick and Cool.** A considerable amount of children who were born during 1970 through 1990 are products of parents who were addicts of the crack generation, when crack cocaine was an enormous epidemic. These children were born in the era when crack cocaine was invented and when the use of this illicit drug was at its peak. This is when many children of the Generation X error were conceived and were unfortunately born into an epidemic of crack babies.

These crack babies were allowed to be born with no questions asked. They were allowed to be born in a world where they couldn't function normally because of their drug addiction at birth. These crack babies were withdrawn from the world, didn't know how to show normal emotions, didn't know how to love or be loved and became extremely violent at early ages. During early childhood and adolescence these crack babies were slow at learning, therefore developing the syndrome of low self esteem, no self worth. The crack babies of this error are now grown up and are in the age range of 35 and younger. Now a days they test young mothers before the babies are born to make sure that they do not have crack or other hard drugs in their systems.

The crack cocaine error also caused many good working people to lose their jobs, homes, families and themselves due to the addiction of this drug. Unfortunately, still today it is an epidemic and causes the breaking up of families, the loss of jobs, homes, etc. Also due to this error many of the children did not have a father figure in their lives because they were incarcerated due to drug abuse, which is still a dilemma of today. We must realize that the father is the engineer of the family, and without him the family will not function adequately.

Generation X as parents

The young parents of today are out of control. We cannot really blame them, for we the older generation are the blame. Many of these children were taught by example, acting out as their parents did.

They were born into a world that is full of foulness, a world that is manipulated by the evil one, a world which is experiencing **Spiritual Warfare** at the peak of its existence. Even more sadly, they are not aware of it.

Because of the times that we live in, many of the children of this generation were brought up self centered, lazy, spoiled, angry, and materialistic. Sadly they were born in an age of worldly concepts through television, radio, newspapers, magazines, books and the internet. Through these concepts they were taught negative information, which followed them into adulthood and they are passing those concepts onto their children.

The majority of this generation hasn't a clue who **God** is or what he represents. They have no connection with our **Lord and Savior, Jesus Christ** and know nothing about religion. Couples don't stay married for any length of time. There is no courtship in newfound relationships. There is no commitment in relationships. To be truthful there are few one on one relationships period.

Predators – Children of Generation X

The children being raised by Generation X as parents are completely off the hook, unless they are living by **God's** word. Children are products of their environment; therefore many children whom are products of Generation X, have poor examples to follow. These young parents talk to their children with foul mouths, cursing at them, yelling at them, calling babies stupid MF's, stupid B's, and so on. They drink in front of them, use drugs in front of them, disrespect them, and talk down to them. Which leads to self hate, low self esteem, and no self worth being installed into their children's personalities before they reach 5 years of age.

A considerable amount of the children of Generation X are labeled as Predators and have no respect for themselves or anyone they encounter with. They start using foul language at 2, 3 and 4 years of age. The sad thing about it is that their parents think it's **Hip, Slick and Cool** to see a small child talk with a foul mouth. By the time these children are 7 or 8, they are talking to their parents, teachers, neighbors and anyone else they encounter, with foulness that you can't believe. These children show no respect for their parents or any other adults, because of their upbringing.

Due to hormones and additives being put in the food that we eat now days, many of these children reach puberty and are promiscuous at an early age. The little girls want to dress like hookers at 7, 8 and 9 years of age. Some start their ministration, develop breasts and develop pubic hair around that same age.

"911"

There is no discipline in the homes today because the government has taken over family values; there are very few fathers in the home for the same reason. The government has made laws enforcing that parents cannot discipline or spank their children calling it a form of child abuse. When in reality not disciplining your children is a form of child abuse. It is stated in the Bible; "Spare the Rod, Spoil the Child."

I'm not condoning child abuse or the beating of children. Unfortunately there are parents and caregivers who brutally beat children causing bruises, burns, cuts, black eyes, broken bones and some eventually kill children from abuse. When it comes to situations of this extreme of course law enforcement should step in. But unfortunately there are parents who are mentally ill in this world, and more sadly, in many cases, these types of situations cannot be controlled.

Children learn about calling 911 at an early age. When it comes to the family unit this number is family genocide. If a parent gives their child a spanking or let's call it what it is, a whopping, for being out of line, these children of today call 911 because they know they have the bluff over their parents, and therefore can do almost whatever they want to do, and won't get in trouble for it. Children are aware that if their parents put their hands on them in the "wrong way" that they can go to jail for it. The more you hold back the rod, the more disrespectful, violent and disobedient the child becomes and the fewer morals they receive.

Because of this government control of the family, parents use verbal abuse instead. Parents holler and scream at their children. They call them names and belittle them. And in turn the children do the same to the parents because they feel they can get away with it. So the children and parents have yelling matches. The children curse their parents out while intimidating them, threatening to whoop their behinds, because they feel as if they have the bluff over their parents.

<u>Children of today are blinded by receiving the wrong information</u>

Yes the tables are turned in the family unit. Children don't listen to positive advice from their parents because they don't have to; they feel as if "they know it all". "You can't tell me anything", is there attitude. If an outsider tries to feed them positive information they tell them to shut up, "You're not my mama", or" you're not my daddy".

I remember back in the day when children were taught to respect adults. When adults were in a room, children were not allowed to enter into that room without permission. Now day's children hold conversations with adults as if they are adults themselves. Back in the day, adults were addressed by children as Mr. Brown, Mrs. Brown, Uncle Bob and Auntie Louise. Children would automatically help elderly people with their groceries, escort them across the street, etc. Children would love to hear old time stories told by the elderly, and would respect them and learn from them. Now days, elderly people are afraid to try and school these children because they may get jumped on, stabbed or shot.

These children suppress their intelligence and their talents because they want to be **Hip, Slick and Cool,** in order to fit in. Instead of being intelligent they will act ignorant because the world around them is foul and dark. The enemy has organizations which are camouflaged, to provide wrong information, therefore manipulating children's minds to live foul, use foul language, to do drugs at extremely early ages, to be angry, violent, materialistic, and disrespectful. These children are being manipulated by the powers of this dark world, not by accident, but by design. They are in the concept of **Spiritual Warfare**, evil at its worst.

Conditions of the Schools – Predators – Children of Generation X

One reason children don't like going to school (in the inner city), is because of the poor conditions of the schools. The school buildings are raggedy and need to be painted; the bathrooms are nasty to the point where the children don't want to use the facilities. There are no books in the schools; there is a limited supply of materials and a limited amount of teachers. The conditions of these schools cause the children to be turned off on learning. Their attention spans are getting shorter and shorter.

While attending school these Predators are out of control. Many teachers have no power over their classrooms. The children talk to their teachers with foul language. They have no respect for them or themselves. The children have no drive or compassion to learn in order to reach their potentials in life. They have the mindset that nobody cares about them; therefore they develop learning disabilities, because their focus is not on learning.

These children will "cuss each other out" in class rooms, and will fight at the drop of a hat if they don't like the way another student looks at them, if another student touches them accidentally, if they are jealous of another student, and so on. If you ask one of them why they are so violent, why they like to fight and disrupt others, they will tell you because "my mother's violent, so I am too, or, my father's violent, so I am too. Any form of violence seems to turn these children on because they were born in the age of mind manipulation, which they encounter on a daily basis.

A major reason why children act out in school is because our government took worshiping **God** out of the school system. They made it a law that children cannot use **God's** name in the classrooms. They once removed **God's** name from the Pledge of Allegiance, but fortunately it was retrieved. The government tried to remove "**In God We Trust**" from our currency. The evil one does not want our children's focus on **God**. He wants them lost in this dark world. In the dark mind set of believing the illusion that **Hip, Slick and Cool** is the way to live, when in reality it is the way to die.

The teachers are intimidated to a point where they pass these children along just to get them out of the way. Unfortunately our government agrees with this concept, and has therefore enforced a law that "no child shall be left behind". In other words who cares if our children adapt to their capabilities. More time is spent on teaching students how to pass an exit exam in order for them to graduate, rather than on academics.

Many of the parents of these children (generation X parents), don't get involved with their children's education; be it joining the PTA, etc., they leave problem situations in the hands of the school board.

Un-Employment - Predators - Children of Generation X

The un-employment rate is steadily on the rise. There are fewer and fewer jobs available for the youth of today. Teenage jobs are scarce for the black youth and black men in this society have been in a struggle trying to find employment for a long period of time. Unfortunately in the times that we live in, black women are in the same boat.

But don't get discouraged. During times like these our father **God** is waiting and willing to help those in need. All he wants us to do is rely on him. All we have to do is know **God** will see us through all of our problems, if we trust and have faith in him. Remember that you can be successful at anything you desire through faith, knowing that **God** through **Jesus Christ** will make a way out of no way.

Don't give up on trying to make an honest living. Don't use the **Hip, Slick and Cool** syndrome, thriving in the darkness of this world through joining gangs, drug dealing, stealing, robbing, pimping, prostituting, conning people, and doing anything foul that you can think of in order to survive. This approach in life will only end in disaster, either landing you in jail or to an early grave. Stay positive and use your imagination. Think of people's needs and necessities and put your thoughts into action. If you think it, you can do it.

There are many services that the youth of today can do in order to make an income. Neighbors and friends always need their trash cans taken to the curb, their porches and driveways swept and hosed down, items from the grocery store, their children picked up from school, baby sitters, hair braiders, going to the laundry mat, painting fences, watering lawns, watering plants, etc.

With just a little thought, you can make a business for yourself. Just be humble, pleasant and use a positive approach. Also have drive and determination, knowing that through **God's** grace and favor, you can accomplish whatever comes into mind.

Computer/Video Games

Computer/video games are designed to promote violence, mayhem, abuse and disrespect. Many of these games are violent beyond measure; featuring pimps and whores, people being shot to death and getting their heads blown off, people screaming from being attacked, people using foul language, people being stabbed, cars crashing and turning completely over with blood squirting all over the place, and any other form of violence you can imagine.

These games are designed to put subliminal messages in our children's minds, while putting an image of violence in their sub conscious minds. Teaching them to be violent, teaching them that living foul is **Hip, Slick and Cool**. Violent computer/video games; another trick by the powers of this dark world to promote evil. Not by accident but by design.

Childhood Obesity

Promoting these computer/video games also contributes to the obesity of our children. All children want to do in this day and age is watch television and play computer/video games. Many children of today have no drive, no energy and are extremely lazy. You practically have to bribe a child to make them go outside and play. They sit around watching television, playing games and eating snacks. They may not move out of one spot for hours, when they should be playing outside and burning calories. After they eat their dinner they lay around and watch television. Which is why numerous amounts of children are obese, and which is why our children suffer from high blood pressure, sugar diabetes, heart problems and cancer.

Many parents of today don't have time to prepare proper nutrition for their children. In this fast paced world that we live in parents go to stressful jobs, then have to deal with road rage, train rage, or bus transportation rage. They come home tired, have to help the kids with their homework, and by the time they are finished they don't have the energy to prepare a decent, healthy meal. Which is why not only the children of today are obese, the parents are also.

You see 4 or 5 fast food restaurants on every corner. Many families live on fast food, for breakfast, lunch and dinner. These foods are heavy in food preservatives, which are salty and are not nutritious. They also contain chemicals that are detrimental to our health. "You are what you eat" and these fatty foods affect the way our children think and learn.

Unfortunately, the government has also eliminated many of the sports activities in the schools, which help our children stay fit. Sports activities build character, sportsmanship, builds up self esteem, and gives children the ability to strive harder. The government has also removed programs that teach art, dance and music from the schools, which handicaps many talented children from achieving greatness. The children of today have no after school activities, such as teen posts and after school social events. Which is why many of them join gangs, just to have something to do, somewhere to belong.

Back in the Day

When I was a child back in the 1950's, food was healthy. There weren't so many preservatives in our food; fast-food restaurants were not in abundance. Very seldom did we eat fast foods. Our parents gave us cod liver and caster oil on a weekly basis to keep us healthy. Now it's very hard to locate these items at the stores. We ate healthy home cooked meals. The family ate their dinner together at the dinner table. We were healthy and happy. We played outside from morning until night, therefore getting plenty of exercise. We hated to be confined in the house. You very seldom saw an obese child, and children didn't have elderly people's diseases.

Life in general was different back then. There was a family unit. Usually there were fathers in the home. If not fathers a solid male role model was around, be it a step father, your mother's solid boy friend, an uncle or your grandfather. Parents were allowed to discipline their children and children grew up with respect for their elders. You could leave your door unlocked. There were no bars on people's windows or doors. Neighbors looked out for each other. The whole neighborhood knew each other by name. People were not materialistic. There weren't so many stresses in life.

The school system was solid for all nationalities. If you didn't pass, you stayed behind until you did. Parents didn't play around with children, and children stayed in their places. There wasn't so much violence, and the world wasn't a bad place to be. I feel sorry for the youth of today. I feel sorry that they have to deal with this dark world that we live in. Only **God,** through **Jesus Christ** can save us from these dark times. There is no other way!

<u>Youth of Today – Don't Give UP! There is HOPE!</u>

Our children of today, (Generation X and the Predators - children of Generation X), feel lost with no hope in sight. They live in a world of darkness, a world that doesn't care about their existence. Throughout their lives they have experienced a great deal of mistrust in our society. Our children are mixed up by receiving the wrong information. Our children witness homosexuality on a regular basis. Our society condones the gay lifestyle. The world today sets the illusion in our children's minds that this lifestyle is the way to be, that it's **Hip, Slick and Cool.**

The government gives our youth the impression through wrong information that marring the same sex is normal. It is written: Multiply and be fruitful. It is a fact that two men cannot father children and two women cannot impregnate each other. The powers at be will use any concept they can conjure up to manipulate the minds of our children in order to go against the grain of **God.** Not by accident but by design.

I believe that many people are born gay. I believe that the human body is not always accurate in the amount of hormones a child conceives when being formed in their mother's womb. That's why women have facial hair, men have hips and breasts, homosexual men have too many female hormones, and homosexual women have too many male hormones. In many instances people become gay due to rape, incest, and child abuse. Then there are those who are gay by choice. Many people are sex addicts, and will have sex with anybody and will do anything to pleasure the flesh. The truth of the matter is, being gay is a fight of the flesh through **Spiritual Warfare.**

If you ask a gay person if they feel like their preference of life is normal, many will say that they don't want to be gay, that it is not easy living the life of a gay person, that they didn't choose to be gay, but they can't help it, "I was born this way". We have all witnessed a child, maybe your little brother, sister or cousin, who at an early age could not identify with their gender. Innocent children who would state: I want to be a boy (when they are a girl), or I want to be a girl (when they are a boy). To be gay is to have sexual desires for your same sex.

Don't get pulled into being gay because other people do it or because society says it's OK. This is why **God** says to "Protect your eyes and ears". You must not trust everything you see and hear. Don't try it because you are curious. Realize that being curious about having sex with the same gender is another ploy by the evil one to take your mind off of **God,** while manipulating it in order for you to concentrate on fleshly desires.

Don't get pulled into being gay because of the way society glorifies that lifestyle. It is not an easy lifestyle to live by. The only way to fight any fleshly desire is by believing and having faith in **God,** praying, confessing your sins, and turning your life over to **Jesus Christ**. Just as our father **God** can remove all addictions, he can also remove all desires. You must believe in the power of our father **God**. You must believe that **God** can do anything and that he is in control of everything.

People born with Transgender Syndrome

People who are born with transgender syndrome are in a different category than people who are born gay. They are in a mind frame that is different from being gay. At an early age the transgender syndrome takes its toll on innocent children. This way of thinking begins when they are 1½ to 2 years of age (before they are able to speak). These children believe that they were born with the wrong sexual organs. They believe their fairy **God** mother will eventually fix them.

If they are a boy child they have mannerisms of a girl and at times have facial features of a girl. They are gentle and meek and want dainty items that a girl would prefer, such as admiring the color pink, ruffles and lace. When they are put in boys clothes they will adjust them by unsnapping their paints to make it a dress, or will prefer loud colors and short pants.

When the transgender boy becomes able to talk and you ask him," are you a boy"? He will politely tell you, "no, I'm a girl". In their minds they truly believe that they are a girl and don't understand why they were cursed with a penis. They truly believe that when they grow up, they will be like mommy. They believe they will have breasts, a vagina and will be able to have children of their own.

The same applies when a girl child is born with transgender syndrome. The girl child really believes that she is a boy. She sometimes has facial features of a boy, has male tendencies, and has the desires of a boy.

Gay children will say, I want to be a girl or I want to be a boy. Transgender syndrome children will tell you, I am a girl or I am a boy. Gay children act out and except their gender. Gays are sexually attracted to the same sex and in most instances except their sexual organs.

Transgender children blame **God,** feeling that he made a mistake and gave them the wrong sexual organs, and therefore hate to acknowledge them. There have been circumstances where transgender boys hurt themselves by trying to remove their penis, or when transgender girls hurt themselves trying to remove their breasts.

It is heart retching to witness children who are born with transgender syndrome. When they reach puberty they become suicidal in many instances because they cannot function normally in society. They truly fill that they are trapped in the wrong body, that they are living in hell.

More than likely the transgender male or female will take hormones during puberty, and eventually have a sex change in adulthood in order to live, what they believe, a normal life.,

Gods Mercy

I believe **God** will have mercy on his children who are born gay and his children born with transgender syndrome. I believe **God** understands their struggles in life. I believe that if it is possible for people to be born with deformities; such as four legs, two heads and both sexual organs. That it is also possible for people to be born with an abundance of the wrong hormones or with deformities in their minds.

The Media – Negative Mind Manipulating Entity - Promoting Racism and Self Hate

The Media is another organization which has our children mixed up by exploiting manipulative, negative, violent, depressing and racist news. While promoting self hate, no self worth and low self esteem to the poor and inner city youth in America.

The Media per trades a certain race of people as perfect, beautiful, non violent, law abiding citizens, that everyone should want to be like. On the other hand singling out other races of people, mainly the poor inner city people, as violent, trouble makers, gang bangers, robbers and murders.

The truth of the matter is there are beautiful people in every race. There are poor people in every race. There are people who live in poverty, are violent, murders, gang bangers, robbers and trouble makers, in every race. The media turns race against race. It manipulates the poor to fight amongst each other, grabbing for crumbs thrown out from the rich.

SPIRITUAL ADVICE TO THE HIP SLICK AND COOL

Setting these images in our children's minds is a ploy by the powers at be, to promote self hate, low self esteem, and no self worth to certain races of people. The media is a mind manipulating organization who promotes racism on a daily basis. Unfortunately the media reaches our children's thoughts and sets illusions in their minds of hopelessness, emptiness, no need to strive, and no future ahead.

The media per trades certain neighborhoods as crime infested ghettos. There are crime infested ghettos in every city. They are not excluded from certain races of people. When murders or robberies occur in "certain areas" You hear people say" I can't believe it happened in this area" Why not? One area is no different than any other area when it comes to crime. Crime does not stop because of your zip code. The media wants you to believe that only certain races of people are poor. There are poor people in all races.

The media mainly per trades people who are poor being busted for committing crimes. The media mainly focuses on the county prison system where the poor are housed, which is considered the blue collar criminals. Why don't they exploit the white collar criminals? Why don't we hear about the white collar crimes? The media should expose the white collar criminals because they rob our country of millions of dollars and set our economy back. Or is it another form of racism?

The media exposes small drug dealers who cell rock cocaine on the streets for $10 - $50.00 a hit. Why don't they expose where the cocaine comes from, or who distributes these drugs to the small drug dealers? The media exploits the poor, while protecting the rich, no matter what they do or how they become rich. This country we live in thrives on wealth.

The media sets the illusion in our children's minds that the more money you have the more power you have. It sets the illusion that the more designer clothes you possess, or the more bling-bling that's around your neck or on your fingers, constitutes your status as a person.

The media projects people who have good looks as being more acceptable. They set the image that the thinner you are the more attractive you are. The media per trades that if you are poor in wealth, that you are a low in class, and have no hope or future in life.

Then we wonder why our children are off the hook. If you look deep, you'd understand why. The media sets an illusion in our children's minds that living foul is **Hip, Slick and Cool.** While manipulating their minds into believing that using foul language, disrespecting women, young women dressing like hookers, young men and women gang bangin, using drugs and possessing an abundance of material items, is the way to live your life. The media in itself is a concept of **Spiritual Warfare**, promoting evil over good.

The media also uses high education as a weapon. If you don't have some sort of educational degree, you can't make a decent living. Unfortunately this stands to be the truth. I remember back in the day when people would hire you with a high school education. They would give you a chance to prove yourself. There would be instances when a person with a high school education would actually rise to the top of an organization, becoming President of that organization.

You see anyone can be trained to do a job, and do it successfully. I'm not saying all professions can be accomplished without a college degree. We need doctors, nurses, lawyers, scientists, psychiatrists, teachers and people of that stature, who must go to college. But those who do not choose to attend college shouldn't be forced to have a college degree in order to make a decent living.

The powers at be designed the education process in order to discriminate against the poor who cannot afford to go to college. Unfortunately today certain colleges discriminate against students of minority status who do qualify and can afford to attend certain colleges. The system is designed to keep the minority or poor man down so they won't prosper. The system is designed to keep the rich man rich and the poor man poor. Not by accident but by design.

The media per trades most people of status as looking a certain way. The media sets the illusion that per trades a certain nationality of people as being the model of how we all want to look like and be like. The media has the entire world in the mind frame of self hate in some form or fashion. We must realize that wealth does not constitute a person's worth. And we must also realize that **God** made us all unique and we should love and appreciate our uniqueness.

We will use **Jesus Christ** as an example: **Jesus Christ** was a poor man while here on earth. He was poor in wealth, but rich in spirit. He was homeless. **Jesus** didn't judge people on their education. He didn't have a college degree. He didn't care about material possessions. **Jesus Christ** spent his time on earth spreading love and compassion. The media per trades **Jesus** in one image when in reality, **Jesus Christ** did not have white skin, blue eyes and blonde hair.

As it is written "His hair was white as wool, or as snow, and his eyes blazed like fire, his feet shone like brass that had been refined and polished". (The Revelation 1 verse 12)

We Are One!

Our children must realize that there is no superior race on this planet earth. **God** made us all equal. **God** made the creation of man from one man. We are all one big family. There is no black race versus the white race. We are all the same race of people. Some people are extremely lighter and some are extremely darker. The color of your skin shouldn't matter, but in the society in which we live in, it does.

It's what's inside your heart that counts. Young people must believe that no one is better than you are, and you are no better than anybody else. Realize that the amount of money someone has doesn't make them a better person than you are. Realize that the way someone looks on the outside, doesn't make them a better person than you are. Realize that the higher someone's education status is, doesn't make them better or even smarter than you are.

I'm not knocking education, intelligence can take you a long way in life, but everyone can't be highly educated. Young people, realize that a large portion of education comes from your father **God**. If you believe in yourself and have faith in **God** you can accomplish anything. Wisdom is the highest knowledge there is, and wisdom comes directly from **God**.

You must recognize your talents and use your abundance of common since, which can make you achieve greatness in life, and you must trust in **God**. Your character is what counts. **God** will give you THIS DAY, your daily bread. Which means everyday you will receive what you need in order to survive for that day. The spirit of **God**, through **Jesus Christ**, which is within us all, is what will make you not only successful in life, but will bring you peace and happiness.

Words to the Wise

Generation X and their children, the Predators, don't fill X'd out. Don't give up on life. There is hope for you. Protect your eyes and ears. When you see or hear evil coming, fight against it with your armor of protection that **God** provides. **Hip, Slick and Cool** is not the way to live your life. Don't get sucked into believing that it is. Use your Wisdom, Insight,

Common Sense, Talents and Instincts to your best advantage, they are gifts from **God,** and will take you a long way in life. Believe in yourself and you can achieve anything you want. **God** will provide all your needs, wants, and desires, if you trust and have faith in him.

Young people realize that however you look on the outside doesn't matter. Be thankful for the wonderful way **God** made you. Respect your parents, your elders, and yourself. Realize that being **Hip, Slick and Cool** is a ploy designed by the evil one, to manipulate you into living as foul a life as possible. Look around and notice how blessed you are compared to some. Don't desire to be or look like someone else. **God** made us all special. He loves us all. Faith, compassion, respect, and love for others, inner beauty, and generosity are traits from **God.** We should live our lives loving one another.

It is written: Love your neighbor as you love yourself.

STORY 8

SPIRITUAL WARFARE/JUST BECAUSE YOU SEE MY TEETH, DON'T MEAN I'M SMILING AT YOU

How many times has someone smiled in your face and stabbed you in the back? How many times has someone smiled at you, and you knew in your heart that the smile wasn't sincere? How many times have you seen a smile turn into a frown?

"Just because you see my teeth, don't mean I'm smiling at you!"

There are two songs whose lyrics remind me of the above phrase:

<u>The Back Stabbers</u>

There smiling in your face, all the time they want to take your place, "the back stabbers"

<u>Smiling Faces</u>

Smiling faces sometimes pretend to be your friend; smiling faces show no traces of the evil that lurks within.

"Just because you see my teeth, don't mean I'm smiling at you!"

You must condition your heart to recognize the evil around you. Realize that the mind frame of **Hip, Slick and Cool** puts out negative energy. Understand that it's not OK to mislead or to lie and deceive people.

How many times have you been betrayed by someone whom you thought was your friend? How many times have you trusted someone with all your heart, only to get stabbed in the back by them?

Evil and negativity is sometimes camouflaged by smiles, hugs, false acts of kindness and acts of concern.

Trust the feeling in your heart. If it doesn't feel right, it's not right.

Smiles

A genuine smile from someone is heartfelt and makes you automatically smile back. It worms your heart and reaches your soul. It gives you a feeling of joy. You feel good all over your body. It's radiating, and touches your holy spirit.

An evil smile from someone makes you feel uncomfortable. You know in your heart that it's unreal. It gives you an on, than off feeling. Look into the eyes of a person when they smile at you. The eyes are the soul of their existence. Eyes never lie.

Hugs

When a hug is genuine it makes you feel good. When it's a good hug, you actually don't want to let go of the person you're hugging right away. A good hug brings peace to your soul, a smile on your face, and comfort in your heart.

A fake hug feels as if you're hugging a log. You feel no emotion from the person you're hugging. You feel no warmth, no connection. Watch out for negative feelings.

False Acts of Kindness

You ever hear the saying: "You don't get something for nothing"

SO NOT TRUE!
There is no price on true kindness. Kindness comes from the heart through the spirit of **God**. Being kind is a loving act. It should make you feel good to be kind to someone else. You should expect nothing in return.

People perform false acts of kindness in order to hold the favor over someone's head. They feel that doing something without charging someone for it, gives them power over the person that they did the favor for. A false act of kindness has a motive behind it. The act is done for selfish reasons: "Now you owe me", "remember what I did for you"?

Acts of Concern

Sincere acts of concern are felt from within the spirit of your heart. When someone is truly concerned about your well being, you can feel their passion. They show affection, are kind, and are positive. They give you comfort by a hug or a gentle touch. You can feel their sincere heartfelt desire to help or comfort you.

False acts of concern also has a motive behind it. I'll help you, if you pay me back. Or the person reminds you over and over again of the help that was given. There is no compassion, no love, no hugs or positive energy for the person who needs comfort.

Remember!

"Just because you see my teeth, don't mean I'm smiling at you"

It is important in our everyday lives that we keep our antennas up and recognize when someone is sincere when they give you a hug, a smile, an act of kindness or an act of concern. Keep your eyes and ears open at all times. Don't be phony. Pay attention to eye contact. The eyes are the windows to our souls and the soul of our existence.

Keep **God** first in your life. Try to always keep a positive attitude. Be a light in this dark world. Remember, you have to recognize **Spiritual Warfare** first hand. You cannot learn the concepts of **Spiritual Warfare** by studying it in a classroom.

If you don't have our **Lord, Jesus Christ's** spirit upon you, you will never be able to recognize the difference between good and evil. It's like dancing in the dark.

Words for the wise: Do unto others, as you would have them do unto you.

STORY 9

SPIRITUAL WARFARE/PLAYERS

Spiritual Warfare exists in our everyday lives. Therefore you must protect yourself from the evil one and understand what is taking place in this dark world. You must also realize that there are organizations which try to persuade you to follow the evil ways of this world. Organizations that are designed by the devil to convince you that being **Hip, Slick and Cool** is the way to live your life, when in reality being **Hip, Slick and Cool** is an illusion of grander designed by Satan to ruin your life.

There is a function called the Players Ball which takes place every year. This function is designed by an organization of pimps, prostitutes, drug dealers, thieves, and cut throats. This function is a mind manipulated event set up by the evil one to promote pimping, whoring, being a thief, being a thug, and drug dealing. Setting an illusion in your mind that living this life style of foulness is glamorous and exciting. When in reality living this life style is immoral and degrading.

The attendees of this function drive up in their fancy cars and limos. They fall in with their floor length mink coats and mink hats, with gold teeth in their mouths, flausing the bling-bling, in tailor made suites like you've never seen before. All the pimps have 3 to 4 or more women; all arm in arm, grinning from ear to ear. Setting an illusion in your mind that this is the good life; setting the illusion that foul living is **Hip, Slick and Cool**. You must be aware of what's taking place in this world. Understand the trap that is being set for you. Understand that all foulness in life comes from Satan.

SPIRITUAL ADVICE TO THE HIP SLICK AND COOL

<u>The Pimp</u>

A pimp is as manipulative as the devil himself. He's like a vampire that sucks the blood out of the living, or shall I say the half living. You see a pimp himself is a coward and a weakling who more than likely cannot fend for himself. In most cases he is uneducated, has learning problems, and is a low achiever. In most circumstances he is also a hater of women. He's more than likely someone who was abused by a women during his childhood. So he uses women to do his dirty work and controls them by fear. Which results in physical, mental, emotional, and verbal abuse.

He takes advantage of people with low self esteem, no self worth. He prays on women who are low achievers, women who feel unloved, unattractive women, women who have been molested, abused, are on drugs, young girls who have run away from home, and any other lost soul he can manipulate. He has a mindset that disrespecting and degrading women is **Hip, Slick and Cool.**

A pimp sets his trap for these elements of people, and then comes in for the pray. He's nice to them at first. He gives them a place to live, feeds them and makes them feel comfortable. He takes them shopping for clothes and other needs and necessities. He gets their hair and nails done and makes them presentable.

Then once he has them depending on him and has softened them with his charm, he moves in for the kill. He first enters their hearts and then captures their minds. He starts playing on their insecurities. He makes them once again feel low and worthless. Makes them feel that they cannot function without him. Manipulating their minds to do anything and everything he tells them to do.

Much sooner than later these unfortunate women start selling their bodies for money to please their master. Turning tricks seems to give them a sense of power. Turning tricks gives them an illusion that the game they are playing is **Hip, Slick and Cool**. When in reality they are playing Russian Roulette with their lives. At first turning tricks seems easy because that's how the devil designed it to be. Then one day they run into someone who wants more than sex from them. They may run into someone who likes to beat prostitutes, or someone who likes to tie them up and stick foreign objects into their private parts. There are also times when tricks will not pay for the favors given.

So they go to the pimp with no money expecting him to understand and have mercy on them because they were put in a trick bag. Not in this game! In the pimp game there is a quota that you must bring home to your pimp every night. There is no mercy given by the pimp if his money ain't right, no matter what happened to you. It doesn't matter if you come home stabbed, beaten up, butt necked, blind, crippled and crazy; you must meet your quota. Because if you don't, you are in for a beating and thrown back into the street to make his money.

The prostitute takes chances being murdered on a daily basis. She may get into a car with a crazy person who pulls out a gun from under their seat. They may get robbed out of their trick money by gun point; pistol whipped, or made to pleasure their abuser for free. Or they may have the misfortune of running into someone who likes to kill prostitutes for pleasure. Someone who feels like a prostitute is a worthless nobody, and who cares if they are dead or alive. This is when you find them dead in hotel rooms with their throats cut, or find their dead bodies thrown into trash cans. Do you think a pimp cares about what happens to these unfortunates? Yes he does, because he is out of some money. All he really cares about is getting paid. In cases like these, he will just go out and get himself some new bait.

The truth of the matter is, if a prostitute gets killed, their blood is on the hands of the pimp. For whatever evil you do in life for the love of money, one day or another you will have to pay for those ill-gotten gains. Be it through a down fall or misfortune, or through a bad accident affecting a family member, or a child getting sick, or something bad happening to them. You won't have a rainbow over your home. Pimps, players, hustlers, cut throats, drug dealers, and other low lives of this world must realize that Satan will make you a slave, and then put you in your grave after he's through using you.

Satan will make you feel like you are in charge, that you are bigger than life. Then when everything is going in your favor, the forces of evil will show up with their calculated moves. The evil one is designed to do what he does, and that is to manipulate, deceive and destroy. Sooner than you think you will end up crossed, either by losing your life or by taking someone else's life.

If you choose to live in the world of the dark, you will find an illusion from the evil one around every corner you turn. Evil forces manipulating your mind while trying to trick you out of your life. You can't win the battle against the evil one under those neon lights.

SPIRITUAL ADVICE TO THE HIP SLICK AND COOL

The Prostitute

As the evil spirit, prostitution has been around since the beginning of mankind. Therefore prostitutes are classified in many categories.

There are women who believe they were born to be prostitutes because of their body structure. Women who feel that their small waists, large hips, big behinds and big legs are designed to sway men into paying attention to them and therefore desiring them, which is usually correct. There are women who love to be controlled by men. There are women who love to give men money. There are women who are nymphomaniacs, therefore love to climax all of the time, and feel like they might as well get paid for it. Then, there are women who feel turning tricks with men is easy money.

On the other hand, there are women who have low self esteem, and feel the only way men will have sex with them is because they are prostitutes. There are women who have no drive or potential in life, so they feel prostitution is the easy way out. There are women who have been sexually abused and are confused about love versus sex. There are young girls who have no direction in life, so they choose the life of prostitution. There are married women who want excitement in their lives, so they choose prostitution for fantasies and exhilaration, and the list goes on and on.

There are also many forms of prostitution: Call girls, nude dancers, phone sex operators, hookers that stand on street corners, wives charge their husbands for sex, crack/meth heads turn tricks for drugs and alcoholics turn tricks for alcohol. Unfortunately there are times when mothers choose to turn tricks in order to feed their children, and the list goes on and on.

Living the life of a prostitute is no joke. It can be a hard life; it can also be a fairly easy life. There are prostitutes also known as call girls that have a cliental of men whom they feel they can trust, so they see them on a regular basis. These women, depending on the class and status of their cliental, can make a good living as prostitutes because they have a steady flow of business, and don't have to go out and pick up strange men off of the street. There cliental is more than likely maintained by word of mouth. But they too are in danger of getting robbed, raped or killed at any given time by their tricks. Because they never really know who they are dealing with.

Street prostitutes put their lives on the line every time they turn a trick. They stand on street corners all alone in the wee hours of the night with the intention of getting picked up by anyone who shows them favor. These prostitutes get into cars with complete strangers; turning tricks in alleys and in the back seats of cars, or going into motel rooms not knowing if they will live to see another day.

A prostitute must realize that they are under Satan's spell. They are under the illusion that being a prostitute is living the good life, when they aren't living at all. They are choosing a death sentence over life. Being manipulated by the evil one to degrade their whole existence. They must realize that they are being driven by the concept of **Spiritual Warfare.**

Prostitutes: Don't be fooled by the evil one. Choose life over death. Don't be blinded into believing that turning tricks is **Hip, Slick and Cool**. Don't be pimped and played, being used by the forces of evil. The evil one is pimping you. You are selling your soul to the enemy.

<u>Drug Dealers</u>

Drug dealers are the scum of the earth whose main purpose in life is to prosper from someone else's misfortune. They too are living in the realms of **Spiritual Warfare**, driven by the evil spirit of Satan. A drug dealer is a power seeker who has the illusion that they are the big man, a big shot, **Hip, Slick and Cool**.

If their sack is large they are able to buy expensive clothes, fancy cars, nice homes, and of course the bling-bling. All elements of making them feel as if they are on top of the world, controlling things. When in reality they are being driven by Satan, destroying the lives of others, and on their way to destroying their own life.

Satan gives drug dealers the false impression of having power over others people's lives. Drug dealers take advantage of people who choose to medicate themselves with drugs in order to fill that emptiness inside their soul, that void that cannot seem to be filled. The misfortunate's feel that drugs will take away the feeling of loneliness and despair. When in reality drug use extends your problems by also taking away hope, drive, determination, goals, potential, purpose, and spirituality.

Drug dealers are the worst element of **Spiritual Warfare,** promoting evil at its best. They strive on making money by poisoning, enabling and taking advantage of people who are unhappy, weak, insecure depressed, products of low self esteem, no self worth, and innocent naive children.

Some drug dealers inherit the drug game handed down from generation to generation. Some do it for kicks because it makes them feel larger than life; it makes them feel **Hip, Slick and Cool**. Some like living on the edge, they like the game of darkness, taking chances with their lives. Some feel it's an easy way to make money. It comes fast, but you best believe it goes just as fast.

Some are good at it, some are not. Some make big money, most don't. Getting robbed from time to time is also a part of the drug game. Some come back from it, most aren't able to. Sooner or later they all get busted and therefore have to pay for those ill-gotten gains one way or another. Some spend years or even life in jail. Some make it down the block and some don't make it.

So you're balling. You're the big time dope man. It's all good in life, so you think. You possess an abundance of material items, the bling-bling, and live high on a hill, drive expensive cars, and keep a bank roll in your pocket. You have more women than you can count on your hands and feet. You walk with your head up in the air, your behind don't even stink. You're on top of the world. That is until Satan puts you in a trick bag and shows up with his calculated moves!

Cocaine happens to be your drug of choice to sling. Being that you taste it when you cop, you start dippin' in your dope sack. Tasting a little here, tasting a little there, until you eventually develop an appetite for it. Then you start rubbing it on your gums to get a little freeze. Eventually you start chippin', dippin' and tooting a little powder to go along with your cognac.

You now have a little monkey on your back, but you feel you're not hooked. Even though you know how the drug game goes you continue to chip and dip in your product until eventually you pick up a crack pipe. One addiction leads to another addiction.

Even though you know what this drug does to people. Even though you've ruined hundreds of people's lives. You feel it can't happen to you, you're too **Hip, Slick and Cool** to get hooked. So you hit the pipe every now and then, and the monkey gets bigger and bigger. Until eventually you become a full blown crack head.

Now you're sure enough hooked, and you know it. But you continue to sling, believing in your heart that you have your addiction under control. Much sooner than later you've become your own best costumer.

Now you're smoking more than your selling, then you just buy dope to take care of your own habit. You start losing weight and don't keep up your appearance like you use to. The women with class slowly disappear. They have no use for a broke crack head. You eventually have to move down in class. Now the crack whores are your new hang out buddies.

Eventually you start taking the bling-bling to the pawn shop. You lose your home, car, and every material item of value. Now you're stealing to support your habit. You don't eat, don't bathe, and you are now in the state of depression. Wondering what happened to turn your life upside down.

Satan - Yes Satan does what he does. He is a liar, a thief and a deceiver, whose main purpose is to trick you out of your life. Your back is up against the wall. What do you do? **Spiritual Warfare** has taken its toll on you. In life you have the power to choose **God** or Satan to rule over your life, good or bad, life or death. So far you've chosen a death sentence. You see - you reap what you sow, nothing good will come out of drug dealing.

Many drug dealers feel as if their backs are against the wall. They feel what choice do I have? I have to make a living. I'm uneducated, unemployed, hated by all races of people, discriminated against, what choice do I have?

What choice do you have? Good Question!! You have the choice to choose good over evil. You have the choice to be on **God's** team. You have the choice to use your free will and choose to clean up your act, in order to find **God's** plan for your life. But first you must be still, listen to **God,** and believe and trust in him. **God** will fight your battles. **God's** power is awesome.

Seek ye first the Kingdom of God and his righteousness and all these things will be added onto you. You must put **God** first and foremost in your life.

Form a relationship with **God.** That is the most important thing in life. And repent your bad deeds to our father **God** through our **Lord and Savior Jesus Christ,** asking him for forgiveness. Humble yourself, don't worry, let **God** worry for you. For **God** is the antidote to worrying. Let go, let **God.**

Words of Wisdom

If you feel someone has low self esteem and no self worth. Lift them up, give them proper guidance, and help them find the light within themselves. Don't take advantage of them; don't feed on someone else's misfortune.

SPIRITUAL ADVICE TO THE HIP SLICK AND COOL

Realize that we are all children of **God**; therefore you will be rewarded for all of the positive things you do in life.

In a life filled with the spirit of **God**, you can go as far as the horizon. There are no limitations to what you can achieve. If you believe it, you can achieve it. Have faith in **God**; set your goals high, work hard, and you can accomplish anything that comes into mind. We were all born in this world for a purpose. **God's** will is for us to love each other, and to help one another understand the importance of positive forces.

In Satan's dark world of **Hip, Slick and Cool,** you can only go so far until you eventually hit a brick wall. Don't be fooled by the negative forces of **Hip, Slick and Cool.** Open your eyes to Satan's trickery, lies, and deceit, before it's too late. Please understand that turning your life over to **God** through **Jesus Christ** is the only way out of game playing. Only **God** can take you out of the darkness and deliver you into the light, the light, which is the **Holy Spirit of God**.

Be aware that you are being driven by **Spiritual Warfare**. Know that **God** gives you the power to choose between the forces of good and evil. You cannot straddle the fence between the two. You're either on **God's** team or your on Satan's team, there is no in between. **God** did not create you to live a foul life. Repent your sins to your heavenly father. He will in turn provide all of your needs. The more you rely on **God,** the weaker the evil forces will be upon you. Trust in **God** and he will give you mercy. You can, if you choose, live a life of love, happiness and have peace of mind.

STORY 10

SPIRITUAL WARFARE

MY RELATIONSHIP/FRIENDSHIP

I, as most women in this world, fight against the evil spirits of jealousy, insecurities, and making assumptions.

I recently got married to a loving man who respects me, is not a dog, shows me affection, and cares about my feelings and desires. My husband is tall, dark, and handsome. He is charming, well mannered, courteous, a gentleman, and a true man of **God.**

I know with all of my heart that he loves me. He tells me he loves me day in and day out. He also shows his love by making me laugh all of the time, keeping me happy, and he puts my feelings ahead of his own. He can feel in his heart when I'm sad or when something is bothering me, and he shows concern.

I couldn't ask for a better man in this day and age. I know that he is a blessing from **God.** I know **God** put him in my life for a purpose. There is no doubt about it. There is no room for **Hip, Slick and Cool** in our relationship. We are devoted to each other, and always put **God** first and foremost in our lives.

Butt....The evil demon of jealousy, insecurity, and making assumptions comes into focus every chance it gets. The devil is always busy. He doesn't want to see people happy and at peace in relationships. As the sane goes "Misery wants company".

Even though I know how much this man loves me, I allow the evil spirit to tell me that he is not sincere. I allow the devil to whisper in my ear "Look at your man lusting at that woman", "He doesn't really love you". Knowing in my heart that he truly does.

When the evil spirit hits you can feel it in your bones. It's an uneasy feeling, an uncomfortable feeling, an evil feeling. If a feeling is not pleasant, nice, kind, gentle, and loving, it is not the spirit of **God**.

You must learn how to recognize the difference between negative and positive energies. It's an ongoing battle between good and evil, which is the concept of **Spiritual Warfare**. It is easy to allow the evil spirit into your mind because it is constantly being manipulated by it. But your heart is filled with the spirit of **God.**

So I bite......I allow the evil spirit to enter into my mind. I start asking my husband questions. Do you like that woman? Does she hit on you? Have you hit on her? Do you sneak around with her? I find myself asking these questions knowing in my heart that this is not the true nature of my husband.

In turn the assumptions trigger him. He gets mad and lets his guard down (which is the Holy Spirit), he starts yelling at me. "Why are you asking me these questions?" "You know I don't chase women". "What can she do for me when I'm in love with you"? "I'm tired of you accusing me of messing around with other women".

THE DEVIL HAS ACCOMPLISHED HIS GOAL

Yes, the devil has accomplished his goal. Through mind manipulation he caused a loving couple to conflict. He caused confusion and mistrust. He turned good into evil.

Then...after we both cool down, we realize that it wasn't either of our faults that we argued. We realize that the conflict began due to the evil one manipulating both of our minds and causing confusion.

We must learn to recognize evil thoughts being manipulated into our sub conscious minds. Anger, frustration, foul language, sadness, arguing, and bad vibrations are all negative energies, which come from the evil one.

Spiritual Warfare is an ongoing battle. You will on occasion allow the devil to enter into your mind. But you must fight the negativity, because you have the power to choose what you want to think about. Listen to your heart which is filled with the spirit of **God.** For **God** is love.

So remember…If you receive a negative thought in your mind, fight the feeling through prayer. Eventually, if you trust him, **God** will remove all negative thoughts. Turn your life over to **Jesus Christ** our **Lord and Savior** and he will fill your heart with the **Holy Spirit,** and put your mind at peace.

FRIENDSHIP

Be very careful when choosing friends and associates. Don't choose people who are in the **Hip, Slick and Cool** syndrome. Don't hang around people who are worldly, such as; people that get high, party all the time, use foul language, disrespect others, materialistic people, liars, cheaters, deceivers, thieves, people who are vain, self-centered, negative, and un-godly. Remember - birds of a feather, flock together.

It is wise to choose friends and associates who are practicing and living by **God's** word. Friends and associates whose spirits are in the light, not the darkness of this world. Choose positive, trustworthy, humble, pleasant, generous, and un-materialistic people who possess inner beauty.

Don't take true friendship for granted. Finding one friend is a gift from **God.** If you find one person who has these qualities in your lifetime, you are truly blessed. Don't let them out of your life, and treat them with the utmost respect, loving them as you love yourself.

It is written:

If you are polite and courteous, you will enjoy the friendship of many people. Exchange greetings with many, but take advice from only one person out of a thousand. When you make friends, don't be too quick to trust them; make sure that they have proved themselves.

Some people will be your friends only when it is convenient for them, but they won't stand by you in trouble. Others will fall out with you over some argument, and then embarrass you by letting everyone know about it. Others will sit at your table as long as things are going well; they will stick to you like your shadow and give orders to your servants, but they will not stand by you in trouble. If your situation takes a turn for the worse, they will turn against you, and you won't be able to find them anywhere.

Stay away from your enemies and be on guard against your friends. A loyal friend is like a safe shelter; find one, and you have found a treasure. Nothing else is as valuable; there is no way of putting a price on it. A loyal friend is like a medicine that keeps you in good health. Only those who fear the **Lord** can find such a friend. A person who fears the **Lord** can make real friendships, because he will treat his friends as he does himself.

STORY 11

SPIRITUAL WARFARE/SELF HATE

Self hate is a strong insecurity designed by the devil to make you feel bad about yourself. The evil one will trick you into hating yourself. He will manipulate your mind into hating the beautiful creation that **God** made. The evil one will trick you into hating your essence, your whole being, your looks, body structure, hair texture, skin color, facial features, and your total existence.

In our lifetime we have all known a person who's said: "I Hate Myself". I wish that I was rich, I wish that I was smart, I hate the way I look, I wish I could buy this, I wish that I could buy that, etc. etc.

How? How can you hate yourself when **God** blessed all of his children so abundantly?

Every human being on earth has one or more features that are beautiful. Everyone has a talent or several talents which can take them a long way in life, if applied through hard work and guidance. We are all blessed with multiple capabilities which allow us to fend for ourselves.

But we must first be satisfied and grateful for the abundance of blessings we receive on a daily basis. We must realize that through **God's** grace we wake up every morning, and also through his grace and favor we are blessed to receive everything we need for that day. Everyone is not going to be rich, well educated, good looking, and own an abundance of material possessions. But we are all special in **God's** eyes. He loves all of his children. The ugliness of this world is not made by **God**, it is made by man.

This material world in which we live in has people believing that the more money you have, the higher in class you are as a person - WRONG

Or...The more education you achieve, the more blessings you'll receive - WRONG

Or...The better you look (on the outside), the happier you will be - WRONG

Or...The more material possessions you own, the more fulfilled you'll become - WRONG

People with an Abundance of Money

People who are extremely rich are no happier than those with a moderate amount of money. They just have more money, and therefore can buy any material items their heart desires. But - they cannot buy the most important thing of all, and that is Love. **God** is love, and if you don't have **God** in your life you will not possess true happiness.

We must realize that the love of money is the root of all evil. Of course money is a necessity in life and good to have, but if you achieve riches and wealth by the hands of the devil by means of manipulation, selling drugs, prostituting others, deceiving others, committing genocide, and other means of foul play, you will never find true happiness in life.

In this material world that we live in, having money is an illusion of grander. Rich people are driven by the **Hip, Slick and Cool** syndrome, having the feeling that they can do and get away with whatever they please. The evil one plants in their minds the illusion that having money automatically makes them important and gives them power. They truly believe that those who have a moderate amount of money are less valuable as human beings.

Some people are born into families with an abundance of money and find themselves taking the blessing of being wealthy for granted. They are able to buy anything their hearts desire, and travel anywhere in the world at any given time. They grow up into believing that they are the higher class of people, and people that are not wealthy are the lower class. In most cases they grow up self centered, greedy, lonely, and unhappy. In some cases they become bored with life, and begin to abuse alcohol and drugs, trying to fill that void in their lives. Not understanding what that void is.

On the other hand there are people who become wealthy by using their talents and working hard for their wealth. If they are wise, they are aware that **God** is the main source in life, and his grace is what brought them into the abundance of money, fortune, and fame. You must realize that becoming wealthy or being born wealthy are both gifts from **God**. If you have **God** in your life, you can not only be rich, but also find true happiness, love, joy, and have peace of mind, (that's if you share your wealth with others who are less fortunate than you are). **God** desires all of his children to have an abundance of happiness. But everyone will not become rich or even wealthy in life.

Remember - If you have the spirit of **Jesus Christ** in your life, you are rich beyond measure, spiritually rich. That void in your heart can be filled with love, kindness, gentleness, compassion, humbleness, generosity and peace - which all come free. They don't cost anything. You must love one another and love yourself. Life is a gift from **God. God** is love. **God** through the blood of **Jesus Christ** will take care of your every need, want, and desire. Can you get any richer than that?

The Importance of Knowledge and Education

Even though education is extremely important to achieve, it is not your first priority in life. It is written: **Seek ye first the kingdom of God and his righteousness, and all these things will be added onto you.** It is also written: **Ask and you will receive, seek and thee shall find, knock and the door will be opened to you.** We must put **God** first and foremost in our lives and learn to rely on him. "Faith is the key". By believing in the power of the almighty **God,** you can accomplish anything your heart desires.

It is written: **My people shall be destroyed due to lack of knowledge**. Read your Holy Bible. Take Bible classes and courses. Attend church and listen to the word of **God**. Faith comes from hearing the word of **God**. Study and memorize scriptures in the bible. Learn and understand how important it is to have **God** in your life. Pray and talk to **God** on a daily basis. Rely on your Heavenly Father to give you each day your daily bread. Be spiritually full of the word of **God**. Let go and let **God** take control of your life.

Also knowledge of self is extremely important. First of all you must know that you are a child of **God.** And that you are a part of **God.** Which means that you are capable of accomplishing any endeavor that you believe in. Believe and you shall receive.

Knowing your culture is also extremely important. Unfortunately black people were stripped of their culture, lifestyle, and language due to the power of their rich heritage. So we must teach each other and our youth about the great achievements our ancestors contributed to the entire world. Teach them to be proud of their African heritage. Make them aware that Africa, the mother land, is where humanity originated and that we as a people have so much to be proud of.

Education

You cannot function in this world adequately without proper education. It is important that our children learn about **God**, self, and the basics of education, which consists of: reading, writing, math, science, history, typing, and also in this day and age, to be computer literate.

We must realize that there are thousands of people incarcerated due to lack of education. Lost souls who have missed reaching their potentials in life. Illiterate people who cannot read or write, and therefore cannot survive adequately in this world. They feel that being **Hip, Slick and Cool** is their only way of survival, when in truth living in foulness is not surviving at all. The **Hip Slick and Cool** way of life is a death sentence, which will only lead you to a life in and out of prison or to an early grave.

Please realize that it is never too late to learn and be accountable of self. Realize that through **God's** grace, anyone's life can be turned around.

It is important to realize that being educated does not make you a square or a nerd. Knowledge is power. And if you have **God's** grace along with a good education, common since, wisdom and insight, there is nothing that you can't accomplish in life. And you will have no problem dealing with the darkness and evils of this world.

To achieve a College education is definitely a blessing from **God.** Unfortunately some people aren't capable of going to college, some aren't cut out for college, and some people don't choose to attend college. But if you truly want to go to college you can do so by working hard and knowing that through prayer anything can happen for you. Even if you don't have the funds, don't give up hope, **God** will make a way, out of no way.

If you choose not to attend college, don't be discouraged. An enormous amount of people rely on their common since in order to make a living. Some people are born with an abundance of common since, some are born with a moderate amount of common since. Then you have people who can only learn from reading books, who have a minimal amount of common since.

I have witnessed many people with a moderate amount of education achieve great accomplishments in life. Many who are blessed abundantly with the gifts of Wisdom, insight and common since. Wisdom, insight, and common since can take you a long way in life. This form of intelligence cannot be taught in a classroom, it comes directly from **God.**

Unfortunately, our society doesn't recognize the moderately educated man with an abundance of common since. People who are highly educated believe that they are better, feel that they are above the common man. They feel that if you don't have a college degree, that you are ignorant and trifling and cannot accomplish anything in life. Those with a higher college education look down on those with a lower college education. In our society the more college degrees you have, the more status you receive as a person.

This way of thinking was designed by the evil one for division, and to create conflict. Another way to keep the rich man rich, and the poor man poor. Society designed the school system for the poor to be inferior to the rich. Not by accident, but by design. Most poor people cannot afford to go to college, and also in the time that we live in its getting harder and harder for not only the poor, but also for the so called middle class students to attend college.

Life would be so much easier to deal with if we all understood that a high degree of education makes no one better or even smarter than anyone else. You should never look down on another human being because you feel that you are smarter than they are. That way of thinking comes from the evil one, manipulating minds and therefore causing conflicts which are concepts of **Spiritual Warfare.**

Jesus Christ never went to college, and he was the greatest man that ever walked the face of the earth. **Jesus** didn't concentrate on worldly desires. His main objective in life was to save souls from Satan's grips, and teach people who followed him how to live life relying and having faith in **God.**

You should never feel inferior or dislike yourself due to your educational status. **God** provides all his children with common since and talents. But you must also have drive, determination, and faith in **God**, knowing that through his grace and favor that you will be able to accomplish anything you desire in life.

If you want to thrive in life by achieving a high education, that's all well and good. Knowledge is the key. But never give up on whatever endeavor you choose. Work to become the best that you can be. Whatever you can do special, advance your art to greatness. Go to trade school for that particular field and master it.

Cut through the chase. If you enjoy cooking and are good at it, go to culinary school. If you have the art to fix cars, go to school to be a mechanic. If you're a good dancer, go to dance school and master your talent. If you're a good typist, take computer classes, go to secretarial school, or school to become a word processor or court reporter. If you are good in art, take art classes. Like to play musical instruments, take music classes. Practice makes perfect.

If you are blessed with talents such as: being a good dancer, having a good singing voice, being able to rap, having charisma, whit, charm, walking with a swagger, a pleasing personality, or you are naturally funny; use your blessings to your best advantage. Don't confuse natural talents with **Hip, Slick and Cool**. As long as you keep **God** first and foremost in your life, use your blessings in a positive manner, and don't manipulate or deceive others to achieve greatness, fame and fortune, you will remain on **God's** team.

If you trust in him, **God** will provide all of your needs, wants, and desires. **God** wants you to rely on him. All you have to do is believe and you can achieve. You can accomplish anything in life that you want, if you work hard and strive for it.

<u>Outer Beauty</u>

In the world that we live in, being blessed with outer beauty can take you a long way in life. Yes, being beautiful is a blessing from **God**. Satan was the most beautiful Angel in Heaven, and as we know, he is the most evil entity on the face of the earth. Beauty on the outside doesn't assure that a person is also beautiful on the inside. You will find most people with an abundance of outer beauty to be conceited, judgmental, cruel, self centered, arrogant, and unhappy within their own skin, unless they are filled with the spirit of **God**.

Beauty from within comes from your heart. **God** is in your heart. Which proves the fact to be true. "Beauty is only skin deep". There is nothing more pleasing than a person with inner beauty. A pleasing personality is an exceptional quality. Being nice, kind, gentle, trustworthy, humble and generous are all traits of inner beauty, which come from the heart.

People with extremely good looks are the most insecure people in the world. They look in the mirror and all they notice are their flaws. Their nose is too big, their chin sticks out too far, their lips are too big or too small. Some dark people want to lighten their skin, some white people tan, spray themselves with makeup or apply potions to their skin in order to become darker. Tall people walk bent over to seem shorter, and so on.

Now a day's people go through great measures in order to try and improve their looks. They get Botox treatments on their faces when they notice a wrinkle or if they have several wrinkles. For many elderly people, Botox isn't quite the answer. If their entire face has wrinkles they may choose to have a face lift. For this procedure to be done the plastic surgeon cuts the skin around the entire hair line and on the back of the neck in order to stretch the skin to make it appear smooth once again. These procedures and surgeries are done monthly or yearly because you can't mess with Mother Nature, the wrinkles return to their natural stature.

Some people have their breasts, buttocks and lips enlarged. Some have liposuction done on their thighs, buttocks, arms, legs and any where they can think of in order to remove fatty tissues. Some go to the extreme, having so many surgeries done that they don't even look like themselves, and begin to look like monsters. They spend thousands and thousands of dollars having these surgeries done over and over again, never to be satisfied. **Spiritual Warfare**, the devil is always at work, causing you to have self hate, hating the skin you're in. Realize that you have to love yourself for how **God** made you. No matter what means or measures you take, you cannot make yourself perfect on the outside. The question is; What is perfect?

The devil manipulates your mind to make you believe that having outer beauty is **Hip, Sick and Cool**. He gives you the false impression that if you are common looking or unattractive, that you are undesirable. He wants you to feel bad about yourself. You can be gorgeous on the outside in other people's eyes. People stare at you in disbelief at how beautiful you are. You can receive compliments on a daily basis on you good looks. But the evil one will manipulate your mind, and when you look in the mirror you hate the way you look., which will drive you to the point of having low self esteem. The evil one thrives on you hating the wonderful way that **God** made you.

On the other hand, have you ever witnessed an unattractive person from first sight. But when they opened their mouth and spoke it was like a voice of an Angel talking to you. Or when they smiled at you, the smile was so gentle that it touched your heart, and you looked past their outer looks into their inner soul. You see beauty fades, love lasts forever, which is your true beauty.

Don't beat yourself up because you don't possess the amount of outer beauty that you desire. Don't worship your desires to be beautiful, and don't worship the structure of your body. Your body is to be used for the glorification of **God's** work. Concentrate on your inner beauty, your **godly** beauty which allows you to feel good about yourself on the inside and outside. Trust in **God** through **Jesus Christ**; rely on **God** for happiness and your life will be fulfilled.

Material Possessions

Unfortunately, we live in an extremely materialistic world. A world that is divided into classes, such as: upper class, middle class, and the poor. Our minds are conditioned to look up to the upper class. Therefore believing that the more money someone has the higher status they are as a person. Our minds are manipulated by the evil one to focus on having as many material possessions as possible, conditioned into focusing on worldly things and stuff, rather than on **God.** Conditioned into putting **God** on the back burner of our lives, and focusing on me, me, mine, mine, the way I look, the stuff I possess.

Have you ever known anyone who has taken material items with them to the grave? If the answer is yes; What value did they have underground? Material possessions are not important, they don't matter. They are another illusion of grander conjured up by the evil one to make certain people feel small and others seem large. Another concept of **Spiritual Warfare.** Another way to give people a feeling of low self esteem. Making them want money so badly to buy material items, that they will do anything and everything in order to purchase them.

The devil will manipulate your mind into having the need to show off, so that others can see "the stuff I have". This is why people are driven to steal, lie, cheat and kill for money. The evil one setting the illusion in their minds that having an abundance of material possessions will make them a big shot; make them feel **Hip, Slick and Cool**.

Don't get me wrong. It's good to have money; we can't manage life without it. We can't survive unless we have money to pay or mortgage, rent, have the comforts in life, buy groceries, clothing, maintain our health, etc., all the necessities in life. But it's not important to possess an abundance of unnecessary material items. Don't make them your priority in life.

Take it from the extremely wealthy. Use them as an example, the ones who don't value material items, but instead use their wealth to help others or build and invent materials to make the world a better place to live. These people don't waste their money buying expensive clothes, extremely expensive cars, bling-bling and such. I'm sure they have some nice things, but their priority is not focused on material items.

What's important in life is love. It is written: Love thy neighbor as you love thyself. Don't dwell on what someone else has or how someone else lives. **God** made you so special. Realize that he will give you anything your heart desires if you turn your life over to him through **Jesus Christ**. Fill that emptiness you fill inside with **God's** love, instead of focusing on the needs and desires of possessing material junk. That's all it is, worthless junk.

<u>Who Am I?</u>

Many people hate themselves so much that they wish and desire to be someone else. There are people who will go as far as changing their own image in order to imitate someone else's. They imitate the way another person dresses, the way they wear their hair, how they walk, talk, their mannerisms, lifestyles, and will at times go to the extreme of getting plastic surgeries done in order to take on the look and appearance of someone else.

In most instances when this occurs it's because that person is dissatisfied with the way **God** made them, and therefore feel they aren't good enough just being themselves. This action is a sign of **Spiritual Warfare** at its worst. The evil one manipulating your mind to make you hate the skin you're in. Satan does not want you to be happy as yourself, and imitating someone else will not bring you happiness either.

Then, there are people who will not unleash their **God** given qualities in order to fit in with the crowd. There are people who will shrink to be small in order to be accepted. There are people who will not reach their full potential because it's not **Hip, Slick and Cool** to do so.

When children reach the ages of 9 through 16, they are under a great deal of pressure from other children. During this period in their lives children are cruel to each other. They tease each other, rag on each other's clothes, shoes and hair styles. They insult each other for wearing glasses and/or having braces on their teeth. Children will make fun of other children when they are smart or not so smart, if they are fat, if they are skinny. Many children develop a sense of low self esteem during this time in their lives.

Intelligent children will get poor grades in school rather than achieve what they are capable of. They would rather achieve a C average when they are capable of achieving an A average, only to fit in with the crowd. You should never be an under achiever.

You must utilize all of your blessings from **God.** You must realize that **God** designed you a certain way. Everyone is unique in their own way. No two people are the same. **God** made you special in his eyes. Don't worry about fitting in or what others feel or say about you. It's not important. What is important is your relationship with **God** through **Jesus Christ.**

Jesus is the way the truth and the life. The light inside you is your holy spirit from **God.** Don't allow anyone or anything to put out that light. **God** loves you as he made you. Concentrate on your inner beauty. Be loving, kind, gentle humble, and understanding. Trust in **God** for peace within yourself. If you keep him first, everything will fall into place, and you will be happy and fulfilled in life.

<u>Who Are You</u>

You are a child of **God.** **God** our creator, designed us and gave us life. Life that we take for granted. When we wake up in the morning, **God** wakes us up. Do you thank him first thing in the morning for blessing you with another day? Or do you wake up, rush off to work or school, grab a cup of coffee, a glass of juice, or a bagel, and get to steppin'. Are you too focused on the illusions of this world to take the time out and thank your creator? Are you allowing the evil one to manipulate your mind set on being **Hip, Slick and Cool?** Allowing him to make you believe that money, fame, and fortune are more important than **God?**

Don't be tricked by the forces of evil. Don't allow Satan to manipulate your mind with the matters of the world so that you put **God** on the back burner of your life. The enemy wants to keep your mind clouded with immoral and degrading thoughts, desires, and self hate.

Who are you? You are a child of **God**. **God**, our father, should be on the front line in your life. Therefore you must worship him first thing in the morning, in the daytime, and at night before you go to sleep. Keep **God** first in your life. Protect your eyes and ears no matter what pressure you are under when dealing with **Spiritual Warfare**. Be who you are designed to be, a light in this dark world.

STORY 12

SPIRITUAL WARFARE

As it is written:

<u>Free Will</u>

Don't blame the Lord for your sin; the Lord does not cause what he hates. Don't claim that he has misled you; he doesn't need the help of sinners to accomplish his purposes. The Lord hates evil in all its forms, and those who fear the Lord find nothing attractive in evil. When, in the beginning, the Lord created human beings, he left them free to do as they wished. If you want to, you can keep the Lord's commands. You can decide whether you will be loyal to him or not. He has placed fire and water before you; reach out and take which ever you want. You have a choice between life and death; you will get whichever you choose. The Lord's wisdom and power are great and he sees everything. He is aware of everything a person does, and he takes care of those who fear him. He has never commanded anyone to be wicked or given anyone permission to sin.

Sirach 14 – 16

EPILOGUE

Happy Ending – **NOT…YET!!**……… After finishing chapter 12 of our book, my husband and I purchased literature from our neighborhood library in search of ways to publish our material without too many second and third parties involved. We read our book over and over as instructed by the literature we received. We proofread for errors, grammar etc. We were so excited, so in love, so devoted to each other, and grasping at ideas of how to go about getting the book published.

My husband has a lot of energy and has to stay busy, doing something at all times. He can only relax for short periods of time, and gets board very easily. Now that we were not putting our energies into writing the book any longer, his attention span wondered into doing things of another nature. You see not only does my husband have a problem of drug abuse; he also has a problem of loving to be in the street life, a problem of being Hip, Slick and Cool. The streets have been a part of his life ever since he was a child.

Unfortunately the people in which he knows in the streets are low life's, drug dealers, drug addicts, alcoholics, pimps, whores, hustlers, thieves, con men and con women, people who are Hip, Slick and Cool. The kinds of people he needs to stay away from. But also unfortunately, these are the people that he grew up with, the people he considers his friends. Whenever he cleans his self up and gets off of drugs, he returns to the street, hoping to save some of his friends. Which always ends up the other way around, him returning to the use of drugs. As they say: Lay down with dogs and you'll get fleas.

I'm basically a home body. I can stay at home, listen to music, watch television, cook and clean the house, and make my day out of it. In my younger days I also ran the streets and loved the Hip, Slick and Cool environment, but the streets are no longer the same. There was a time in L.A. when the night life was off the hook. Jazz clubs, dance clubs, and after hour hangouts where an abundance. But now a days there is nothing in the streets but trouble.

My husband eventually returned to the grips of the devil and started back drinking, smoking crack cocaine, and hanging in the streets with low life's. Returning to the life of Hip, Slick and Cool. His addiction reached to the point of no return. He used drugs day and night. He returned to his Dr. Jackal – Mr. Hyde personalities. Again our spirits clashed; my holy spirit apposing his evil spirit – His evil spirit opposing my holy spirit. Spiritual

SPIRITUAL ADVICE TO THE HIP SLICK AND COOL

Warfare at its worst.

After about three months or so of his escalating dependency on drugs, my husband's mind was completely controlled by Satan's lies. Any and everything said or done by me, in his mind, was a lie or a plot against him. He began accusing me of having men in the house whenever he left home. No matter what time it was, these men were waiting around for him to leave so that I would invite them in and have sex with them. In his mind I was having sex with our neighbors, men and women up and down the street, and anyone that looked my way.

Eventually Satan convinced him that I was having sex with his childhood friends. It started out being two of his friends, which he almost considered to be his brothers. Then escalated into three of his childhood friends. Even more sadly he accused me of paying to have sex with them. His friends who had wives or girl friends that I respected. His friends whom were financially stable. His friends whom I couldn't afford to pay to have sex with, even if I wanted to. One of his friends that he accused me of I only met once, therefore wouldn't know him if I saw him on the street. Satan had tricked his mind through his weakness, (the use of drugs) into believing that the people he loved most in the world were betraying him.

He developed a love/hate relationship with me, and dismissed his friendship with his close friends completely. Due to the abundance of drugs my husband consumed, due to him being depressed about what he believed was going on between his friends, the neighbors, and I. He soon developed a paranoia syndrome and became delusional. He believed what he wanted to believe. No matter how I tried to convenience him that I was devoted to him and him only, anything I said in his mind was a lie. I swore on the bible, confessed in church (the house of the Lord) that these things he thought in his mind were not taking place. But he didn't believe me. I never could lie to my husband because I loved him so much. When you truly love someone, lying and deceiving them isn't an option.

I was so hurt that my husband felt this way about me. So hurt that he believed (in his mind) that my personality, morals, and way of life had completely changed. He labeled me as a sorry low life; a liar, a whore, a slut, an insecure piece of garbage that had to pay men to be with me. He labeled me as a person that was weak minded, who was unable to think for myself, a person with low self esteem and self hate.

I tried to convince him constantly that I was the same woman that he fell in love with. That I would never commit adultery because it is against God's will. That I would never hurt him because of the deep love I had for him. That I was a virtuous woman and didn't marry him in order to have sex with his friends. That I never desired any of his friends or any other man besides him. That I don't have to pay men to have sex with me or take advantage of me. That I thought highly of myself. That I knew I was blessed by God, and knew in my heart that I was one of his children.

Once upon a time, every now and then, when he was sober, he questioned himself. He questioned what Satan was feeding his mind. But soon he believed Satan's lies, sober or not. Mr. Hyde had taken over his identity. His mind was no longer his own. He was consumed by Satan's grips. His looks weren't even the same. His demeanor was that of an evil entity. Spiritual Warfare is no joke, and I was living it on a twenty four seven basis.

Eventually he started asking me questions about how and when the infidelities started. I assured him that none of the lies Satan was feeding his mind were true. I assured him that he was going through Spiritual Warfare, but that's not what he wanted to hear.

Next, the beatings began. If I didn't tell him what he wanted to hear, he would come at me like a demon. So I began to make up lies so that I wouldn't get beat up. But he would beat me anyway because he believed the lies I told him, and couldn't bare the hurt and pain in his heart. His heart hurt tremendously when he was high or sober. When he was high he couldn't enjoy being that way because his entire thoughts were triggered on my infidelities. Spiritual Warfare, the devil was at work. He cried, was depressed, and talked constantly to his low life friends about the lies Satan was feeding his mind, then badgered me because he felt these low life's judged me as being a whore. Not by my actions, but by what he had told them.

He threatened to kill me on a daily basis. I was in fear of my life and in constant agony. I cried twenty four seven. I was a nervous wreck. I couldn't make noise when he was at home because he believed I was letting men in the house, or that I was looking at them or talking to them out of the window. All the lights in the house had to be on, and if we were in the bedroom the door had to be locked, because he thought I'd allow men to enter into the house at any given time. I had to be in the same room as he was. If I went to the bathroom or kitchen he would follow me. Whenever the phone rang he believed I was talking to another man, setting up a date.

My husband would hold me hostage preventing me from going to work. He prevented me from taking my grandchildren to school. He prevented me from being out of his sight, because he believed whenever I left the house that I was meeting one of his friends.

No matter what measures I took to prove to him that what he thought wasn't true, he wouldn't believe me. In my husband's mind and soul, what he thought was true. I was living a complete lie, admitting that everything he accused me of as being the truth, because if I didn't, I was in for a beating.

Eventually, he wouldn't leave the house without me being with him. And when he did leave me alone he would call constantly, accusing me of having men there while he was on the phone, and would beat me when he came home. I hated being with him when he was high because I'd have to hang with him and his friends (the low life's) all day and night. Riding around in the car searching for another hit or trying to hustle money for another hit. He would be little me and have me begging people for money. This was after he took any and all of my money. And when my money ran out, I'd get badgered and beaten. If he didn't have crack cocaine, he would drink any and everything. Unfortunately alcohol gave him the same violent affect.

When he was under the influence of alcohol or crack cocaine, the devil would intensify his anger about my infidelities. He would start asking me questions, and if I didn't say what he wanted to hear (which were lies), he would beat me in the car while I was trapped with the seat belt on. He would badger me and verbally abuse me, disrespect me in front of his low life friends, and treat me like I was garbage.

Why did I stay with him? "FEAR" my husband knew I was afraid of him and he played on it. You see fear comes from the devil, and my husband had become a product of Satan. "Spiritual Warfare", Satan had taken over my husband's mind through his weakness for drugs, because he knew he was special and a child of God. Satan knew my husband was a danger to his dark world because of his wisdom, insight, and knowledge of spiritual warfare. Satan knew my husband and I had written a book on spiritual warfare. And that we were in the process of spreading the word of God and the evil temptations and mind manipulations that the effect of spiritual warfare has on God's children, who aren't aware of it. Satan did not want our book published. Satan's next target was me, my demise, by the hands of my husband.

Why did I stay? Because of the love I had for my husband. Because I knew who my husband was before he allowed Satan to tempt him with drugs, his weakness. I knew the man I married was under Satan's grips. I knew in my heart that one day my husband would wake up and break the spell of Satan's lies and deceit. I knew my husband loved me, and that God would fix him, in his time. I realized that we were being tested and living what we wrote in our book. I knew we had to walk in the shoes of "spiritual warfare" in order to speak about it thou rally.

The abuse became unbearable. I couldn't take it anymore. God will only give you as much as you can bear, and I was at my breaking point. I had no joy. I hated my life to the point where I didn't want to live anymore. I gained at least 25 pounds and couldn't lose any weight due to stress, and due to the fact that I ate to medicate the pain I was suffering. I looked horrible and began to age. I didn't care about my appearance. I was in a deep depression with no hope in sight. My fear was progressing. I had to walk around on pens and needles, scared that my husband would suspect something if I moved the wrong way or made the wrong sound around him. I sat at the same spot on my bed crying and praying, crying and praying, asking my father God to please save me from the hell in which I was living. Remember: God only helps those who help themselves. I had to learn to rely on him. But not yet!!

Not only was I stressing, but my daughter, my son in law, and my grandchildren were stressing. Afraid that my husband would sooner than later land me in the hospital or kill me. My son in law wanted to physically hurt him because of the pain he caused me. I have two grandsons who adore me, and I couldn't imagine the pain they would bare if something drastic happened to me by the hands of my husband. My daughter and son in law begged me to leave my husband because of the love they had for me, and I took them up on the idea because of the love I had for them. I couldn't allow them to continue to suffer because of my weakness of staying in an abusive relationship.

The first time I left home, I only stayed away for a couple of days, and he talked me into returning home. Then I'd stay away 3 – 4 days at a time, which turned into a month. He called constantly. He left threatening message after message. I paid the rent because one day I was planning to return home, which I did. My husband promised that he would stay sober. It lasted about seven days and he returned to using drugs.

Satan was steady feeding my husband's mind foulness and lies. My husband confronted me saying that I was spending my time with one of his friends during the time that I stayed away from home. He suggested that his friend ordered me to come back home, so I obeyed. He believed that his friend was in complete control of me. In other words his friend sent me home to get abused and I said "OK, I'll go home and get beat", anything you say. My husband believed that his friend and I were using drugs together, and I was paying for them. He accused me of giving his friend thousands of dollars at a time. (Where I got all this money – I don't know). He accused me of buying his other friend a new car. (I needed a car myself). Of course the abuse continued.

I left home again and stayed away for another month. This time he was happy that I was gone and made our place the crack party house. Crack whores were sleeping in my bed, and coming and going as they pleased. They were using my things, taking my things, and having a field day at my expense. I continued to pay the rent and utilities, again planning to return to my home. He got used to the single life and began to enjoy me not being in the way. I told him that I was returning home one day and he was not happy at all about the idea. I returned home, just for spite, and he made me as uncomfortable as he possibly could. I stayed one day and left again.

I finally filled for a restraining order so that I could return home and remove him from the premises, (so I thought). When you file a restraining order you cannot serve it yourself and you have three weeks for it to be served by someone else. Therefore it was hard for me to get someone to serve him. He wouldn't answer the door and I couldn't locate him when he wasn't at home. I ran out of time trying to serve him with the restraining order therefore had to file a revision.

This time I had the police serve the order. I waited outside our home until I knew for a fact that he was there, called the police on my cell phone, and they served him. He was ordered to leave the premises and not to return. (Yeah right) a restraining order is only a piece of paper which couldn't initially keep him away from me and he knew that. I called myself moving back home, but that was a joke. I had no home; our place had become the devils den.

FEAR!!! I lived in fear twenty four seven. I changed the locks on the doors. I was a nervous wreck, whether inside the house, while entering the house or attempting to leave the house. My heart jumped every time the phone rang. When I escaped from the house, I felt as if someone was following me where ever I went. I steadily looked over my shoulder, with everyone looking to me as being suspicious. I had no peace. While at home, all I did was cried and prayed, cried and prayed, asking God what I had to do in order to have peace in my life.

Whenever he called, he would threaten to kill me, my daughter, and my grandchildren. Or have me beat and killed by someone else. I would become so fearful from his phone calls that I would leave home and go over to my daughter's house. I spent more time over her house than I did at home. I was always scared to go home by myself. I would either take someone with me or I'd call the police to escort me home.

Eventually my husband began stalking the house. If he caught me coming out, he would kidnap me and keep me in the streets with him or he would hold me hostage at home. The beatings in the car and at home escalated. My husband believed that I was in love with his friends and that it was their ideas to have him put out of the house, change the locks, and have him served with the restraining order. He believed that I was giving his friends all of my money and that we were buying drugs with my money. One day after staying over my daughter's house for a couple of days, I came home to a paint can being thrown into my front window. Luckily it was water based paint, and I was able to clean up most of the mess.

My husband had become a full fledged demon. "Spiritual Warfare" He was driven by the devil and had no connection with God. My husband allowed Satan to take over his mind and ruin his life. Satan strived on my husband destroying my life also. Satan did not want our book published. And was trying to destroy us both by any means necessary.

There were many instances when I thought I was going to die. One thing about it, I always knew that my God was with me and no matter what I was going through, he was not going to let this man kill me. God saved my life over and over again. I would continually rebuke Satan when my husband went on his rampages. I would always call on my Lord and Savior. I would repeat – No weapons formed against me shall prosper, the Lord is my Shepherd, I shall not want. I would tell him – God loves you, so do I. When I said these phrases, the devil in my husband would become out raged, but he would back off of me.

My husband kidnapped me and kept me over night once again. I was suppose to take my grandchildren to school that morning so my daughter knew something was wrong when she couldn't locate me. She went to the police station and filled a missing person's report. During those 24 hours, my husband had been hitting me, slapping me; he spit in my face, made me have sex with him, made me beg people for money, kicked me and treated me like a dog because of what Satan continuously fed his mind about my infidelities. He'd hit me in front of his low life friends and felt nothing of it. And they felt like I deserved the punishment for doing him so wrong.

As I said, God was always with me. My son in law went out looking for me the next day. He told my daughter that God was going to lead him to me. He knew where my husband hung out from times when we went looking for him when my husband took my car, and because I showed him his hang out spots. Luckily my son in law found my husband and I while we were leaving one of his friend's houses. God directed him to me. When I saw my son in law, it was like seeing an angel. My son in law threatened my husband to leave me alone, or else.

My husband warned me not to go over my daughter's house and spend the night again, no matter what. But of course that night I did. There was no way I was going home to get abused over and over again.

The next day I went to the police station to file a report and to let them know that I was still alive. I turned around and there he was at the police station. He had the nerve to be filing a harassment complaint against my son in law. He sat next to me at the police station and it was like sitting next to a serial killer or someone of that sort. He was a person I no longer knew. He asked me had I been home, had I seen the place. He said, " I told you not to spend the night out again". I immediately left the police station with two police escorts. They had to make him go back inside because he was following us to the car.

I went to my house with my son in law the next day to find the locks changed on the front door. Luckily the back door was still accessible. When we entered into the house my husband had ram shacked my entire home. Anything that was made out of glass was broken. Glass covered the floor of every room in the house. He pulled the kitchen cabinets apart, pulled the closet doors apart, pulled all of my clothes out of the closets onto the floor, and just had the house in complete chaos. "Spiritual Warfare" If I could have been a fly on the wall, just to see how Satan had him in the state of a demonic craze. I just cried as I was used to doing, and cleaned up the place as best I could.

The last attempt on my life was one night when I went next door to our house to attend a party. After I left the party, I went home to get some things, and he was outside the door when I was getting ready to leave. This time Satan was manipulating his mind, giving him orders to finish me off. This was my night to die. He forced me into the house. I didn't know that he had a weapon under his coat. He threatened to beat me with the weapon, while he cried and made me admit to being unfaithful. I screamed for my life and begged him not to kill me. I had to fight for my life. So I took hold of the object and would not let go. Finally he gave up, picked up another weapon, and made me leave with him.

I knew in my heart that I was in real trouble. He forced me into a car where a man and woman were inside waiting, but then he decided to take my car. He was in the process of taking me to the ATM in order to get whatever money I had out of my account. His male friend and his girlfriend followed us. I again was seat belted and unable to move. Being the coward that he is, he began to hit me in my face and my face instantly became swollen. As we turned the corner, there were police everywhere. Fortunately for me there had been a bank robbery early that evening by our house. As the signal light turned red, I jumped out of the car and ran to the police. As I stated God saved my life over and over again.

Do you know this man turned the car into the driveway in front of the police and told me to get into the car? I yelled and told the police that he was kidnapping me, and that the car he was driving was mine. The police informed me that they could not leave the scene of the crime, that there was nothing they could do but call another officer so that he could take a report.

The officer that took the report had an attitude like "Who cares", "been here, done this a hundred times". After taking the report, he told me to call someone to pick me up. I called my oldest sister. I went over to her house, but I could not rest because my husband had not only taken my car and all of my keys, but he had my purse with all of my identification in it.

I kept my abuse situation a secret for a long time. But fortunately by this time my entire family was aware of me being abused by the hands of my husband. My sister and I picked up my younger brother and we went over to my house. When we arrived my car was parked around the corner. I took for granted that the car was locked, and believed that my husband was inside of the house with my car keys. We called the police in case he was inside.

When the police arrived they checked the car, and fortunately the car door was unlocked with my purse inside. The only thing missing was a few dollars that I had in my wallet. When I entered into the house with the police, no one was there. The police took pictures of my swollen face and the ram shacked house. They filled a report to add to the twenty or so that had been recently filled by me. I then retrieved some clothes, and drove my car to my daughter's house. My cell phone rang, and it was him. He stated that he beat me this last time because of how I talked to him on the phone. I hung up the phone and immediately changed my cell phone number. That was the last time that I saw or spoke to my husband, to this day.

The next morning I notified the owner of the house that I was moving. I let them know that my husband was still occupying the premises, along with squatters who were coming in and out at any given time. I stopped paying rent and had the utilities cut off. I began to secretly move things out of the dwelling when one day I noticed in the mail, correspondence from several lawyers. I knew what that meant; my husband had once again been arrested.

I felt relieved and somewhat safe, but saddened at the same time. I felt saddened because this seemed to be the story of my husband's life, him going in and out of prison. I still felt threatened to go to the house by myself in order to move my things, so I always had someone with me. Do you know the squatters changed the front lock and bolted the back door? When the owner changed the locks, the squatters began to go into the house by entering into the windows. Eventually I moved all of my things out. What a relief!

I received one letter from my husband, and was saddened to hear that he had the same feelings about me. His mind was still being manipulated by Satan into believing that I was a whore. I didn't write a return letter.

I pray for my husband every day. I pray that no harm comes to him. I pray that God removes the hurt and pain from his heart and the lies from his mind, so that he may have peace. I pray that all that's in the dark (lies and deceit) come to light (the truth). I pray that he doesn't hate me for loving him. I pray that he knows I'll always be there for him. I pray this time, that he chooses the right path in life. I believe you only get a certain amount of chances in this world. I pray that he doesn't wait until it's too late. He has to want to be saved. He has to go to God and repent his wrong doings. Only God can save him.

Spiritual Warfare, Hip, Slick and Cool – My husband chose through free will, to allow Satan to manipulate his mind while feeding it foulness. He chose drugs and alcohol to be the main focus of his life. He chose to allow Satan to control his life through the desires of his flesh. My husband chose through free will, to run the streets with low life's, spending days and weeks at a time smoking crack, drinking, and being abusive, not only to me, but to anyone he encountered with. He chose to live a life of Hip, Slick and Cool, which is self destruction, putting God on the back burner of his life. My husband chose through free will, to allow Satan to rule over his life.

My husband chose to be on Satan's team, to make worldly desires his first priority. And because he chose this path, his reward was unhappiness, depression, paranoia, anxiety, foolishness, insecurity, selflessness, misery, and a life of self destruction.

It's ironic why my husband chose this path when he knew better. But from the hurt in his heart that reached all the way back from his childhood, the hurt of being insecure, with low self esteem, and being frightened of this dark world, made him want to medicate his pain and anguish with drugs and alcohol.

My husband was a spiritual man, a man who once loved, and I believe still loves me so deeply. My husband would quote scriptures from the bible at the drop of a hat. My husband knows God's wrath and fears God. He once had a kind, generous heart, and at one time treated me like a queen. There was a time when my husband and I were so happy that it scared us. We knew Satan would interfere with our happiness. Unfortunately, my husband bit and let Satan tempt him into ruining our love and devotion to each other. My husband and I lived for a moment and time the elements of the book that we both wrote. I believe God allowed us to go through hell in order for us to feel the wrath of evilness through spiritual warfare. God wanted us to recognize spiritual warfare first hand. Fortunately I did, unfortunately my husband didn't want to. He did what he wanted to do, and that was to give into his fleshly and worldly desires.

We both knew before all this chaos happened that God had plans for us, and I still believe in my heart that his plans will be met by me and by my husband. Not only will our book be published, but we will both spread the word of God and the awareness of spiritual warfare in order to try and bring as many souls as possible to God, through Jesus Christ our Lord and Savior.

At the moment my husband is once again incarcerated. God removed him from the streets, away from drugs and alcohol and out of Satan's grips. God sat him down so that he can get his thoughts together and make our father God, his first priority in life. God wants his special child back. God wants my husband to once again rely on him, not on the desires of this dark world. God will clear his mind of all of the lies that Satan has clouded it with. God will save my husband, once again.

As it is written: The wages of sin is death. Choose Life!!

CLOSING MESSAGE

May this message reach the core of your soul. Life is like a school course. Each one of us is a student in the school of life. May you be blessed and pass the course when it's your turn to come in front of the **Lord.** Don't allow the powers of **Hip, Slick and Cool** or the temptations of fast money, fast women/men, fancy cars and the bling-bling, entice you into receiving a failing grade for which there is no makeup class.

A hint to the wise should be sufficient; **LOVE** is stronger than any addiction. Everyone goes through their moment of attempting to be **Hip, Slick and Cool.** The point we are trying to make is, that you turn your life over to **Jesus Christ** before it's too late. Protect your eyes and your ears. For the final call is near.

ABOUT THE AUTHORS

My husband Chuck and I were born in Los Angeles. Unfortunately, spiritual warfare attacked us both at an early age. Satan attacked me due to the abandonment of my father who died when I was not even two years old. And attacked my husband due to the abandonment of his father, and due to his inabilities to read as an adolescent. We both chose to fill the void in our souls with the street life, drugs, alcohol and fornication. Because of the path I took, I got robed of reaching my potentials in life at an early age, and because of the path my husband took, his life was a revolving door, in and out of prison. We believe God put us together in the later years of our lives because it took that long for us to learn how to rely on him. God chose us to write this book, and God, through Jesus Christ, will be glorified by it.

www.ingramcontent.com/pod-product-compliance
Lightning Source LLC
Chambersburg PA
CBHW071519040426
42444CB00008B/1715